MILLY-MOLLY-MANDY'S
Things to Make and Do

Other Milly-Molly-Mandy
books from Macmillan

The Milly-Molly-Mandy Storybook

More Milly-Molly-Mandy

Milly-Molly-Mandy's Adventures

Milly-Molly-Mandy's Family

Milly-Molly-Mandy's Friends

Milly-Molly-Mandy's School Days

MILLY-MOLLY-MANDY'S
Things to Make and Do

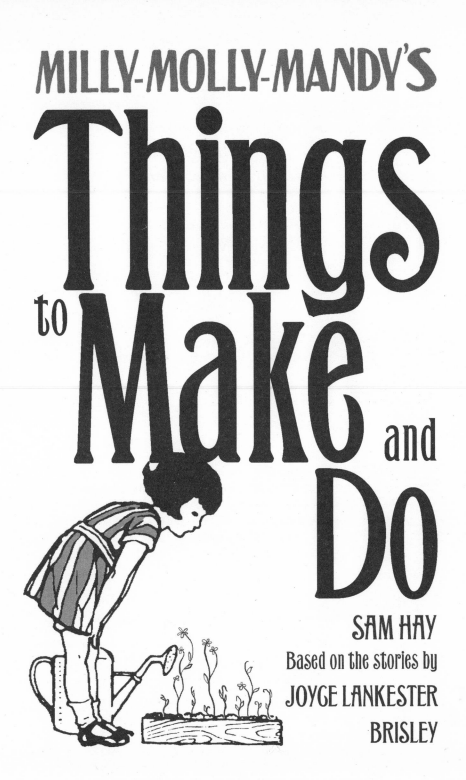

SAM HAY

Based on the stories by

JOYCE LANKESTER BRISLEY

MACMILLAN CHILDREN'S BOOKS

First published 2011 by Macmillan Children's Books
a division of Macmillan Publishers Limited
20 New Wharf Road, London N1 9RR
Basingstoke and Oxford
Associated companies throughout the world
www.panmacmillan.com

ISBN 978-0-230-75494-2 (HB)
ISBN 978-1-4472-0662-0 (Special Edition)

This edition copyright © Macmillan Children's Books 2011
Original text and illustrations copyright © Joyce Lankester Brisley 1928,
1929, 1932, 1948, 1955, 1967
New illustrations copyright © Freya Harrison 2011

Text by Sam Hay. Additional text by Rachel Petty

The right of Freya Harrison to be identified as an
illustrator of this work has been asserted by her in
accordance with the Copyright, Designs and Patents Act 1988.

1 3 5 7 9 8 6 4 2

A CIP catalogue record for this book is available from
the British Library.

Printed and bound in the UK by CPI Mackays, Chatham ME5 8TD

Contents

Introduction

Once upon a time there was a little girl. She had short hair and short legs. But her name wasn't short at all. It was Millicent Margaret Amanda – which was much too long to say. So she was known as Milly-Molly-Mandy . . .

The magical world of Milly-Molly-Mandy is full of old-fashioned fun. Together with her chums Little-friend-Susan and Billy Blunt, Milly-Molly-Mandy is always busy doing something exciting.

From long summer days spent berry-picking and gardening to cosy afternoons in the kitchen learning to bake apple turnovers and cherry cake, there's always something new to do; Milly-Molly-Mandy's great at making something lovely from next to nothing.

Now you can join in the adventures too with this exciting guide to all her favourite things to make and do.

Things to Make and Do in the Kitchen

"Come along, Milly-Molly-Mandy, and have a cooking-lesson with me, it's such fun!"
Milly-Molly-Mandy Gets to Know Teacher

You will often find Milly-Molly-Mandy in the kitchen, learning to make little biscuits or cakes. These simple recipes are ideal for children and grown-ups to follow together.

Comfort Food

When the nights draw in and it's cold outside, a lovely bowl of comfort food is just the thing!

Blackberry and apple crumble

. . . and Milly-Molly-Mandy gathered such a big basketful that there was enough to make blackberry puddings and jam and tarts and jelly and stewed blackberry-and-apple and fresh blackberries for Father and Mother and Grandpa and Grandma and Uncle and Aunty – and Milly-Molly-Mandy too.
Milly-Molly-Mandy goes Blackberrying

This is a lovely autumn pudding to share and enjoy after a hard day's berry-picking.

You will need:
A big basket of blackberries (about 1 lb /400 g)
5 cooking apples (about 2 lb/1 kg)
5 tablespoons granulated sugar
For the crumble topping:
8 oz (200 g) plain flour
4 oz (100 g) butter or margarine
3 oz (75 g) granulated sugar

1. Preheat your oven to 180 degrees C/gas 4.
2. Wash the blackberries (remove stalks), then ask an adult to help you peel and core the apples and chop them into small chunks. Grease an ovenproof dish with a bit of butter. Then put the fruit in the dish and gently mix in the sugar.
3. Make the crumble topping by rubbing the butter and flour together until the mixture looks like breadcrumbs, then adding the sugar.
4. Cover the fruit mixture with the topping and bake for 40–45 minutes, until the top is golden brown. Serve with custard or cream.

❀ ❀ ❀ **TIP** ❀ ❀ ❀
Try other crumbles too: rhubarb, or apple and pear.
❀ ❀ ❀

Blackberry buns

These delicious little buns are easy to make and perfect for picnics or lunchboxes. Experiment with other fruit flavours too: try apple and spice, or sultana and cinnamon.

You will need:
4 oz (100 g) blackberries
12 oz (300 g) self-raising flour
4 oz (100 g) brown sugar (and a bit extra to sprinkle on
    top)
5 oz (125 g) butter (melted)
1 egg beaten lightly
½ pint (300 ml) milk

(Makes 24)

1. Preheat your oven to 180 degrees C/gas 4.
2. Grease two bun tins with butter. Mix together the flour, the fruit and the sugar in a large bowl.
3. Stir in the milk, melted butter and egg. Don't over-stir – you want the mixture to be coarse and slightly lumpy.
4. Spoon the mixture into the bun trays. Sprinkle each bun with a pinch of brown sugar. Bake for about 15 minutes until the buns are browned on top.

Rhubarb jam

"Milly-Molly-Mandy, would you please run up and
fetch me a pot of jam?"
Milly-Molly-Mandy said, "Yes Mother. What
sort?'
And Father said, "Blackberry."
And Grandpa said, "Marrow-ginger."
And Grandma said, "Red-currant."
And Uncle said, "Strawberry."
And Aunty said, "Raspberry."
And Mother said, "Any sort you like, Milly-Molly-
Mandy!"
Milly-Molly-Mandy Has a Surprise

Bread and jam is one of the easiest and most enjoyable things
to eat when you're peckish and in a hurry. Jam might seem
like a complicated sort of thing to make, but it needn't be. Of
course sugar gets jolly hot and can be dangerous, so you will
need an adult to help you.

7

You will need:
1 lb (400 g) rhubarb
1 lb (400 g) caster sugar
The rind of one lemon

1. Wash the rhubarb and remove any stringy bits. Now weigh your rhubarb carefully, as it is important to have the same amount of sugar as you do fruit when making jam.
2. Carefully cut the rhubarb into one-inch (2.5 cm) pieces and tip them into a preserving pan or heavy-based saucepan. Cover with the sugar and place over a gentle heat. Stir continuously to prevent burning. When the sugar has melted completely, stir in the lemon rind and turn up the heat.
3. Boil the jam for 10 minutes, then remove the pan from the heat and allow it to cool down a little. Ask an adult to sterilize your jars for you by putting them in boiling water for 10 minutes, then spoon the warm rhubarb into each jar. Seal with lids.
4. Allow the jars to cool in a draught-free space and remember that once the seal has been broken the jam must be stored in the fridge.

❈ ❈ ❈ **TIP** ❈ ❈ ❈
Don't forget to label your jars with the type of jam they contain and the date you made it. You could make the labels look pretty and give the jars as gifts – everybody loves homemade jam!

Apple turnovers

And when Milly-Molly-Mandy came into the kitchen . . . what did she see but Teacher with one of Mother's big aprons on and her sleeves tucked-up, learning how to make apple turn-overs for supper.

Milly-Molly-Mandy Gets to Know Teacher

These apple turnovers use puff pastry, which makes them lovely and light. Making your own puff pastry can be fiddly, and takes a bit of time and practice to get right. But ready-made puff pastry is ideal and is available from most supermarkets. If you haven't got any, you could use a basic shortcrust pastry instead.

You will need:

4 or 5 medium-sized apples – peeled, cored and chopped into small pieces.

A teaspoon of mixed spice

One block of puff pastry (about 1 lb/400 g)

4 oz (100 g) golden caster sugar

1 oz (25 g) butter

1 egg yolk and a tablespoon of milk mixed together (to glaze)

(Makes 6)

1. Preheat your oven to 200 degrees C/gas 6.
2. Melt the butter gently in a pan then add the chopped apple, sugar, mixed spice and 1 dessertspoon of water. Cook gently for about 5–10 minutes, until the apple softens. (Stir often so it doesn't stick.)
3. Put the mixture to one side to cool. Roll out your pastry on a floured surface. Make a large rectangle shape – about ¼ in (0.5 cm) thick.
4. Now cut into 6-in (15-cm) squares. You should be able to get about 6 turnovers from the pastry. Next, spoon some of the apple mixture into the middle of each square and sprinkle with a bit more sugar.

What did she see but Teacher learning how to make apple turnovers

5. Using a pastry brush or a finger dipped in water, dampen the edges of the squares so that they will stick when you fold them over. Fold over to make triangle shapes. Press the edges firmly together, and make a little cut in the top to let out the steam while your turnovers are cooking.

6. Place your turnovers carefully on a baking sheet covered in baking paper. Glaze with the egg yolk and milk mixture, then add a final pinch of sugar on the top of each one. Now bake for about 20 minutes or until golden brown. Allow to cool slightly before eating.

Shortcrust pastry

And Mother was saying "Always mix pastry with a light hand,"and Teacher was looking so interested, and didn't seem in the least to know she had a streak of flour down one cheek.
Milly-Molly-Mandy Gets to Know Teacher

You can use this basic pastry recipe for lots of different recipes – apple pies, quiches or delicious jam tarts.

You will need:
6 oz (150 g) plain flour
3 oz (75 g) butter, chilled and cut into cubes
1–2 tablespoons of water
A pinch of salt

Rub the flour, salt and butter together until you have a mixture that looks like breadcrumbs. Slowly add one to two tablespoons of water. Squeeze the mixture together into a ball, adding a little more water if it is too dry. Put the mixture on a floured surface and knead gently for a few minutes. (Don't knead too long or it'll become tough.) Wrap in cling film and leave to rest for half an hour in the fridge. Then it is ready to use.

Jam tarts

They had hard-boiled eggs, and brown bread and butter, and cheese, and tomatoes, and buns and a big jam-tart.
Milly-Molly-Mandy Goes for a Picnic

To make jam tarts, roll out your pastry, then use a cutter to make small circles. Grease a bun tin and line with your pastry circles. Fill  each one with your favourite jam – perhaps one you've made yourself! Bake at 200 degrees C/gas 6 for about 15 minutes.

❀ ❀ ❀ TIP ❀ ❀ ❀
You could also try making star-shaped lids for your tarts by cutting out star shapes and laying them on top of the jam tarts before you bake them.
❀ ❀ ❀

Cheese and tomato pies

Bake these little savoury pies in the same way as the jam tarts, but instead of using jam make a cheesy tomato filling. To do this mix up 2 eggs, some grated cheese, chopped tomato and a small amount of milk (about ¼ pint/150 ml). Pour the mixture into the pastry shells and bake for about 15 minutes. When cool, you could decorate with a slice of tomato.

❀ ❀ ❀ TIP ❀ ❀ ❀

If you have any pastry left over, why not make a few funny shaped biscuits too? Use raisins or chocolate chips to decorate and then bake along with your main dish, just as Milly-Molly-Mandy did when Teacher made apple turnovers.

❀ ❀ ❀

Vegetable stew

**But, my! You never tasted anything so good as
that stew!**

**"Well," said Milly-Molly-Mandy at last,
"we can't say we don't like stew, or carrots, or
potatoes, or parsnips now!"**

**"I wish," said Little-friend-Susan, "we could
always cook our dinners ourselves."**

Milly-Molly-Mandy Makes a Dinner

This is an easy and healthy stew that tastes lovely and will
really warm you up on a cold day.

And the onions smelt most delicious!

You will need:

2 tablespoons olive oil

1 medium onion, diced

1 large potato, cubed

Assorted vegetables such as leeks, peas, parsnips, squash, courgettes and carrots, chopped into roughly 1-in (2.5-cm) cubes

1 tin chopped tomatoes

½ pint (350 ml) vegetable stock

Salt and pepper to taste

1. Heat the oil in a heavy-based pan and add the onions. Fry gently for about ten minutes or until the onion is soft.
2. Add your vegetables and fry for a further minute. Then add your tin of tomatoes and stir well.
3. Pour in the stock, cover your pan and leave to cook for about half an hour. Make sure all the vegetables are cooked through by poking them with a fork, then season with the salt and pepper.
4. Serve with bread and butter.

 TIP

You can try adding some barley (add at the same time as the vegetables) or mini pasta shapes (add about 10 minutes before the stew is finished) to make the stew even more satisfying.

Lid potato

There's something very comforting about a baked potato, as Milly-Molly-Mandy discovered after a busy day playing with Little-friend-Susan.

First Mother took two well baked potatoes out of the oven. Then she nearly cut the tops off them – but not quite. Then she scooped all the potato out of the skins and mashed it up with a little salt and a little pepper and a lot of butter. And then she pushed it back into the two potato-skins, and shut the tops like little lids . . . And they opened the potato-lids and ate them with little spoons.
Milly-Molly-Mandy Enjoys a Visit

Baked potatoes are very easy to make. Here's how to do it:

You will need:
A large potato
Butter, salt and pepper to taste

1. Preheat the oven to 190 degrees C/gas 5.
2. Wash the potato and cut off any bad bits. Prick all over with a fork. Pop in the oven for about an hour and a half, or longer if you're using extra-large potatoes.
3. When they are cooked you can eat them the same way as Milly-Molly-Mandy – as lid potatoes. Just make a flap in the top of the potato, scoop out the insides and mix with butter and salt and pepper, then return the mixture to the potato and serve with a small spoon!

Here are some other fillings you could try in your lid potato:

* Cheese
* Ham and cheese
* Salmon and sweetcorn
* Tuna and mayonnaise
* Cream cheese and chives

If you're short of time you can make a lid potato in the microwave. Prick your potato all over with a fork and place it in a heatproof dish. Cover with clingfilm and microwave on high for about 15 minutes.

If you want your potato to have a nice crisp skin then you can ask an adult to grill it for about five minutes to finish it off.

And, my! You never tasted anything so good as those potatoes!
Milly-Molly-Mandy Cooks a Dinner

Pumpkin and ginger soup

Fancy! – a real pumpkin, like what Cinderella went to the ball in drawn by mice, growing in Milly-Molly-Mandy's own little garden!
Milly-Molly-Mandy and the Surprise Plant

Even if you haven't grown your own pumpkin, this is still a great recipe to use up the flesh you've scooped out of your Halloween pumpkin. Waste not, want not!

You will need:
1 tablespoon olive oil
1 onion, finely chopped
 2 cloves garlic, crushed
1-in (2.5-cm) piece root ginger, peeled and grated
1½ lb (600 g) peeled and chopped pumpkin flesh
1½ (900 ml) vegetable stock

1. Sweat the onions gently in the olive oil for 5 minutes, being careful with the hot oil, which can spit.
2. Add the onion, garlic, ginger and pumpkin and cook for 5 minutes more.
3. Add the water or stock and simmer (which is a bit gentler than boiling) for 15–20 minutes, until the pumpkin is tender when you poke it with a fork.

4. Puree the soup in a blender or food processor or use a hand-held blender to do it in the saucepan.

5. Allow to cool a little before eating with lots of bread and butter!

❀ ❀ ❀ **TIP** ❀ ❀ ❀

Learn how to grow your own pumpkin on page 128.

❀ ❀ ❀

Sticky gingerbread

And at five o'clock that very afternoon Milly-Molly-Mandy and Little-friend-Susan and Billy Blunt were sitting drinking milk from three little mugs and eating gingerbread from three little plates, and feeling just as excited and comfortable and happy as ever they could be.

Milly-Molly-Mandy Finds a Nest

This gingerbread is very easy to make and will leave your whole house smelling lovely. It lasts for a long time if you keep it in an airtight container, but only if you can resist eating it all at once!

You will need:
8 oz (200 g) self-
    raising flour
1 teaspoon baking
    powder
3 teaspoons ground ginger
1 pinch salt
2 oz (50 g) butter or margarine
2 oz (50 g) soft brown sugar
8 tablespoons black treacle
2 eggs, beaten and mixed with milk to make ½ pint (300 ml)

1. Preheat oven to 180 degrees C/gas 4 and grease and line a 2-lb loaf tin.
2. Mix the flour with the salt, baking powder and ground ginger.
3. Melt the butter or margarine and add the sugar and black treacle, mixing them together very well. Watch out – this mixture will be very hot indeed!
4. Add your butter mixture to your flour mixture and mix well with a wooden spoon.
5. Gradually beat in the egg and milk mixture to make a smooth, thick batter.
6. Pour into the loaf tin and bake for about 45 minutes, or until a skewer comes out clean when inserted.

"When you go out, Milly-Molly-Mandy, please go to the grocer's and get me a tin of treacle. I shall be wanting some for making gingerbread."
Milly-Molly-Mandy Dresses Up

❀ ❀ ❀ **TIP** ❀ ❀ ❀
Your cake will get stickier the longer you keep it!
❀ ❀ ❀

Sweet Treats

These bite-sized sweets are all perfect to give as gifts. You could make a little box (see pages 249–51) or basket (see page 188) to put them in, or just place them on some cellophane and tie it up with a ribbon.

Coconut Ice

You will need:
2 oz (50 g) condensed milk
10 oz (250 g) icing sugar
8 oz (200 g) desiccated coconut
2–3 drops pink food colouring

1. In a large bowl, mix together the condensed milk and icing sugar using a wooden spoon. Slowly add the coconut until it is mixed in evenly. You might like to use your hands for this part but make sure they are nice and clean!
2. Now you should split your mixture into two equal parts. Knead a little bit of pink food colouring into one of the halves until the colour is even.
3. Dust a board with icing sugar and shape each half into matching, smooth rectangles. Place one half on top of the other and with a rolling pin, push the two together. Use your hands to reshape into a rectangle.
4. Leave uncovered to set overnight or at least for 3 hours.

When it's ready, you can cut your coconut ice into squares and share it with your friends and family!

Sugar mice

And suddenly she saw a tray of pink sugar mice in a sweet-shop, labelled "Two a penny".

"Oh, Mrs Hooker!"said Milly-Molly-Mandy, "would you mind waiting for a moment while I get a sugar mouse to take home to Farver and Grandpa and Uncle?"
Milly-Molly-Mandy Goes Visiting

These are fun to make and are very good to give as presents.

You will need:
1 lb (400 g) icing sugar
Peppermint essence
½ tablespoon lemon juice
2 egg whites
Icing sugar for dusting
Edible silver balls
Thin white string/bootlace liquorice
Pen lid

1. In a big bowl, beat the first four ingredients together until the mixture is stiff and smooth. If it is too dry you might want to add a little water or lemon juice.

2. Now you can shape the mice, making sure you wash your hands first.

3. Dust your hands and a clean board with icing sugar and shape some of the mixture into a pear shape with one side flattened. Don't forget to make a pointed nose for your mouse!

4. Use the end of a pen lid to make holes for the eyes or use edible silver balls. For the tails, make a small dent with the pen lid and push either your liquorice bootlace or thin white string into the hole.

5. Leave your finished mice to dry.

❀ ❀ ❀ **TIP** ❀ ❀ ❀

If you are making some peppermint-cream sugar mice for a birthday party, you could add a couple of drops of food colouring to the mixture to make them a bit more colourful!

❀ ❀ ❀

No-cook fudge

Fudge is so wonderfully sweet that it is best eaten in small quantities – a small bagful is a lovely gift.

You will need:
3 oz (75 g) butter
4 tablespoons condensed milk
½ teaspoon vanilla extract
1 lb (400 g) icing sugar, plus extra for dusting

1. In a big bowl, beat together the vanilla extract, butter and condensed milk.
2. Sift the icing sugar and gradually mix it in. You might have to use your hands to make sure the sugar is properly mixed in, so make sure they're clean. When you are finished, the mixture should come together to form a firm ball.
3. Now you should dust a clean surface with icing sugar and place the ball on to it. With a rolling pin, roll the mixture evenly until it is a square about ¾ in (1.5 cm) thick. Cut this into smaller squares.
4. Leave your fudge to dry overnight.
5. If you are making your fudge for a special occasion, why not cut it with pretty shaped cookie cutters instead of cutting it into squares?
6. To make **chocolate fudge** follow the recipe above and add 1 oz (25 g) of cocoa powder to the icing sugar when sifting it into the mixture.

Rainbow truffles

These colourful little balls would look lovely in a Christmas tray box. (See pages 249–51 for how to make one.)

You will need:
Paper cake cases
2 oz (50 g) cream cheese
3 oz (75 g) icing sugar
2 teaspoons cocoa powder
Hundreds and thousands

1. Lay out small paper cake cases on a baking tray.
2. Beat the cream cheese with a wooden spoon until it is smooth. Gradually add in the icing sugar and cocoa powder.
3. Pour a tablespoon of hundreds and thousands into a saucer. Then make little balls out of the mixture and roll them in the hundreds and thousands.
3. Put the balls into the paper cake cases and refrigerate for half an hour to set.

Toffee

"Mother makes toffee sometimes, with sugar," said Milly-Molly-Mandy. "I wonder if we could!"
Milly-Molly-Mandy Makes Some Toffee

You might not think that toffee is something you can make yourself, but it's actually very simple indeed. Just ask an adult to supervise, as sugar gets very, very hot!

You will need:
A baking tray, approximately 1 in (2.5 cm) deep
Baking parchment
A non-stick saucepan
Butter
A mug
Caster sugar
Water
Brown vinegar

1. Line your baking tray with baking parchment, then rub a thin layer of butter all over it so that your toffee won't stick.

2. Fill your mug with water and pour it into your saucepan. Add 3 mugfuls of sugar and ¼ mug of vinegar.

3. Ask a grown-up to turn the heat on low and stir the mixture until all the sugar dissolves. Then ask your grown-up to turn the heat up and let the mixture boil without stirring it for about 15 minutes.

4. To test if your toffee is ready, carefully dip a teaspoon into the mixture and then into a glass of cold water. If the toffee goes hard, then it is ready; if not, boil it for a bit longer. When it's ready, it will be golden brown.

5. When your toffee is ready, ask an adult to pour it into the baking tray and leave it to set for about half an hour. When it is completely hard, use a rolling pin to crack it into bite-sized pieces, and enjoy!

Chocolate biscuit-cake bites

These magic little cakes don't need any cooking at all!

You will need:
6 oz (150 g) plain chocolate
6 oz (150 g) butter or margarine
1 tablespoon golden syrup
9 oz (225 g) crushed digestive biscuits

1. Line a 7-in (18-cm) square baking tin with baking paper. (Use a small trace of butter to stick it to the sides.)
2. Melt the chocolate, butter and syrup in a pan on a low heat. Mix in the crushed biscuits. (To crush the biscuits, put them in a sealable plastic sandwich bag and bash them with a rolling pin.)
3. Pour the mixture into the tin, allow to cool then put in the fridge for 2 to 3 hours to set.
4. When set, use a knife to cut around the edges, and turn out on to a chopping board. Cut into small squares.

❀ ❀ ❀ TIP ❀ ❀ ❀
Try adding chopped nuts or marshmallows to the mix.

❀ ❀ ❀

Party Food

There's nothing nicer than being invited to a party, except maybe throwing one yourself. These recipes are perfect for eating in between party games!

And then they had supper – bread-and-butter with coloured hundreds-and-thousands sprinkled on, and red jellies and yellow jellies and cakes with icing and cakes with cherries, and lemonade in red glasses.
Milly-Molly-Mandy Goes to a Party

Butterfly buns

And it was such a beautiful little cake, and so nicely browned, that it seemed almost too good to eat.
Milly-Molly-Mandy Spends a Penny

These pretty little cakes are fun to make and ideal for parties.

You will need:
4 oz (100 g) margarine
4 oz (100 g) caster sugar
2 eggs
1 teaspoon vanilla essence
4 oz (100 g) self-raising flour
Paper cake cases
Small jelly sweets to decorate

Butter icing:
2 oz (50 g) soft butter or margarine cut into small bits
3 oz (75 g) icing sugar

(Makes 12 big buns or 24 smaller ones)

1. Preheat your oven to 180 degrees C/gas 4.
2. Cream the margarine and sugar together with a wooden spoon. Then beat in the eggs one by one, and add the vanilla essence. Mix in the flour gradually and stir the mixture until it is smooth.

3. Fill a bun tin with paper cake cases and divide the mixture equally between them. Bake for about 20 minutes, or until the tops are lightly golden and springy to the touch.

❀ ❀ ❀ **TIP** ❀ ❀ ❀
To be sure they're cooked, stick a skewer,
a toothpick or the tip of a knife into one cake.
If it comes out clean, they're ready.
❀ ❀ ❀

4. Leave the cakes to cool on a wire rack. Meanwhile make the butter icing.
5. Sieve the icing sugar into a bowl. Then, in a separate bowl, beat the butter or margarine until creamy. Now combine the icing sugar and butter.
6. When the cakes have cooled, carefully slice off the top of each one, then cut that piece in half to make wing shapes. Spread each cake with butter icing, then arrange the wings on top to look like a butterfly has landed there. Use a jelly sweet for the butterfly's body. To finish, dust lightly with a bit of icing sugar.

❀ ❀ ❀ **TIP** ❀ ❀ ❀
You could also try adding cocoa powder to the butter
icing to make chocolate butterfly cakes.
❀ ❀ ❀

Puff-pastry party twirls

You will need:
Baking paper
Flour for dusting
Ready-made puff pastry
Jam (any sort will do)
Caster sugar

1. Line two or three baking trays with baking paper (this recipe will make about 30 twirls, depending on what size you cut them).
2. Now, on a floured surface, roll out your pastry into a large square, then cut in half to make two rectangles. Spread both rectangles with jam, but leave a space around the edges. Dampen the edges of the pastry using a pastry brush or a finger dipped in water, so that when you roll it up the pastry will stick together.
3. Now tightly roll up one rectangle (lengthways), pressing the end firmly to hold it together. Do the same with the other rectangle.
4. Then wrap your rolls in cling film and put them in the fridge to chill while you warm up your oven to 200 degrees C/gas mark 6.
5. Unwrap your pastry, and chop the rolls into slices about ½ in (1–2 cm) thick.
6. Lay the swirls on your baking sheet, sprinkle with a pinch of sugar and bake for 10–15 minutes. Add another pinch of sugar when you take them out. Cool before eating.

Pinwheel sandwiches

These fun sandwiches use the same method as puff-pastry party twirls, but instead of pastry you use bread. Any soft filling will work.

1. Take a slice of bread, cut off the crusts, then gently flatten with a rolling pin. Now spread your filling on to the bread.

Here are some ideas:

❖   Egg mayonnaise and cress
❖   Cream cheese
❖   Chocolate spread and mashed banana
❖   Grated cheese and Marmite

2. When you've spread on the filling, roll the piece of bread up tightly as though it's a Swiss roll. Then wrap it in cling film and put in the fridge for half an hour (chilling will make it easier to slice).

3. After 30 minutes slice, then secure each wheel by threading on to a cocktail stick and serve.

Chocolate-chip cookies

You will need:
8 oz (200 g) butter
6 oz (150 g) caster sugar
6 oz (150 g) soft brown sugar
1 tsp vanilla extract
2 eggs
12 oz (350 g) flour
1 teaspoon bicarbonate of soda
1 teaspoon salt
12 oz (300 g) chocolate chips

(Makes about 24 biscuits)

1. Preheat your oven to 190 degrees C/gas 5.
2. Cream the butter and sugars together, and then add the vanilla extract and the eggs. Add the salt, bicarbonate of soda and flour slowly, mixing as you go, until you have a creamy mixture. Now stir in the chocolate chips.
3. Squeeze the dough gently into a ball shape, then pull off small pieces to roll into smaller balls – about the size of a small satsuma. Lay them on a baking sheet (leave space around to spread), then press down on them with your thumb to make flat biscuit shapes. Bake for 9–11 minutes or until golden.
4. There are lots of other things you could try in your cookie mix instead of chocolate: dried cranberries, cocoa powder, raisins, chopped nuts or jelly beans.

Delicious Drinks

Cooking needn't just mean food – these drinks will complement any meal.

Sherbert drink

And then there were refreshments – raspberry-drops and aniseed balls on saucers trimmed with little flowers; and late blackberries on leaf plates; and sherbet drinks, which Billy Blunt prepared while Milly-Molly-Mandy and Little-friend-Susan stood by to tell people just the very moment to drink, when it was fizzing properly.
Milly-Molly-Mandy Gives a Party

You can add sherbet to any drink to make it fizz. Try blackcurrant or lemon squash. Just put a few spoonfuls into the drink, stir well and watch the fizz. Here are some other drinks to try.

Old-fashioned lemonade

This drink is perfect for a hot summer day. It takes quite a bit of squeezing, but tastes delicious.

You will need:
¾ cup of sugar (and 1 cup of water to dissolve it in)
1 cup of fresh lemon juice (about 5 or 6 lemons)
6 cups of water to dilute

Makes 6 servings

1. First, make sugar water. To do this, put the sugar and 1 cup of water into a pan and heat gently until the sugar has all dissolved.
2. Use a juicer to extract all the juice from your lemons. Sieve into a large jug to make sure you don't get pips or pith in the mixture, then add the sugar water to your juice. Finally, dilute the juice until you get the taste you want. You can vary the amount of lemon juice and sugar to suit.

Lemonade fizz

Add a scoop of ice cream to a fizzy drink to make it fizz up in front of you. Lemonade and cola work particularly well. Serve in a tall glass with a long spoon to scoop out the ice cream.

Summer-fruit smoothie

Chop a small banana and drop it into a blender with a large handful of fresh strawberries and ½ pint (300 ml) of milk. Blend until smooth. Add a little sugar to taste.

Yogurt cooler

Peel and chop up a pear and put into a blender with some apple juice, a small pot of natural yogurt and a spoonful of honey. Blend until smooth and serve with crushed ice.

Rainbow ice

Here's a fun way to add colour to a drink. Fill a jug with water, add a few drops of food colouring, then pour into an ice-cube tray and freeze. When the ice cubes are ready, add them to drinks and they will change the colour of the drink as they melt.

You could also make rainbow ice cubes by partially filling the tray with one colour, allowing it to freeze, then adding another layer which is a different colour, allowing it to freeze, then another colour. Repeat until full.

Fruity ice cubes

Another fun idea for ice cubes is to freeze fruit inside them. Just pop a strawberry, cherry or raspberry inside each compartment of your ice-cube tray when you fill it up with water. They're perfect for summer parties.

Miniature Magic

It was the prettiest little tea-set with a teapot that would really pour, and a sugar-basin with a tiny lid, and two little cups and saucers and plates – "one for me, and one for Susan," thought Milly-Molly-Mandy to herself. "I'll ask Mother if I can ask Susan to tea today."

So she carried the box into the kitchen (where Mother was busy taking the cakes out of the oven) and asked. Mother admired the tea-set, and said, "Certainly, Milly-Molly-Mandy. And you may have this little cake on a saucer, and one of these little bread rolls to look like a loaf."

So that afternoon Milly-Molly-Mandy laid a small cloth on the garden table and arranged her tea-set on it, with a little vase of flowers in the centre, and all the good things Mother had given her to eat; and when everything was ready she ran down the white road with the hedges each side to ask Little-friend-Susan to come to the tea-party.

Milly-Molly-Mandy Has a Tea-Party

40

Even if you don't have a miniature tea set, you can still throw a tea party using miniature food – perfect for doll-sized guests! You can make smaller versions of all the recipes in this book, or why not ask your mum or dad if they can put some mini food on their shopping list?

Ideas for perfectly sized doll's food:

- ❖ Cherry tomatoes
- ❖ Baby carrots
- ❖ Quail's eggs
- ❖ Pre-cooked mini sausages
- ❖ Little gem lettuce
- ❖ Miniature bananas

Perfect for Picnics

At last they came to the specially nice picnic place.
And it really was almost like a fairy glen, with
daisies and buttercups, and grassy slopes, and
trees to climb, and a little stream running through
the middle.
Milly-Molly-Mandy Goes for a Picnic

As Milly-Molly-Mandy learnt, even the most ordinary food
can taste extra special if you eat it outdoors. Here are some
ideas for things to take along with your sandwiches to make
for a perfect picnic.

Cherry rock cakes

**And Mrs Green cut up a cherry cake into big
slices, and they all had to help to eat it up . . .
Milly-Molly-Mandy couldn't think why anybody
wanted to eat their dinner indoors.**
Milly-Molly-Mandy Goes for a Picnic

You won't need to remember to take a knife to slice up this
cherry cake; this recipe makes 12 individual little cherry buns
and is very simple to do.

You will need:
3 oz (75 g) butter or margarine, plus extra for greasing
10 oz (250 g) self-raising flour
4 oz (90 g) soft brown sugar (plus some more to
    sprinkle on top)
4 oz (100 g) glacé cherries
2 oz (50 g) raisins
1 egg (beaten)

(Makes 12)

1. Before you start, preheat your oven to 200 degrees C/gas 6
   and grease a baking sheet with a little butter.
3. Now rub the butter and flour together until the mixture
   looks like crumbs. Add the sugar, cherries and raisins.
   Add the beaten egg and mix everything together. Use your
   hands to squeeze the mixture into a ball shape. Tear off
   lumps of the mixture to form rough balls, and place on the

baking sheet. Sprinkle each heap with more sugar. Bake in
the oven for about 15 minutes.

Banana honey buns

You will need:
Paper cake cases
4 oz (100 g) butter
8 oz (225 g) self-raising flour
4 oz (100 g) soft brown sugar
7 oz (175 g) raisins
2 eggs (beaten)
2 tablespoons honey
3 ripe bananas (mashed)

(Makes about 24)

1. Before you start, preheat the oven to 180 degrees C/gas 4
   and line a bun tray with paper cake cases.
2. Rub together the butter and flour until your mixture looks
   like crumbs. Add the sugar and raisins, then the beaten
   eggs, the honey and the bananas. Stir together, then spoon
   into the paper cake cases. Bake for around 15 minutes and
   cool on a wire rack.

❀ ❀ ❀ **TIP** ❀ ❀ ❀
To make it easier to spoon the honey out of its jar,
first dip a spoon in hot water – the honey will slide
off the spoon into your mixing bowl more easily.
❀ ❀ ❀

Little Carrot Cakes

She beat the eggs in a basin, and stirred the cake-mixture in the bowl, and after Mother had filled the cake tins she was allowed to put the scrapings into her own little patty-pan and bake it for her own self in the oven (and that sort of cake always tastes nicer than any other sort, only there's never enough of it!).

Milly-Molly-Mandy Goes Sledging

You will need:

4 oz (100 g) self-raising flour
4 oz (100 g) soft brown sugar
2 oz (50 g) chopped walnuts
6 oz (150 g) raisins
4 large or 5 medium carrots, grated
2 medium eggs
6 tablespoons sunflower oil
A teaspoon allspice

(Makes about 12)

1. Before you start, preheat your oven to 190 degrees C/gas 5 and line a bun tin with paper cake cases.
2. Mix the flour, sugar, walnuts, spice and raisins together in a bowl. In a separate bowl, mix the eggs and carrots and beat in the oil. Add the dry mixture gradually to the wet mixture and mix well. Then spoon into the cake

cases and bake for about 15 minutes or until the cakes are golden and springy to touch.

3. For an extra twist, try adding a topping. Mix together icing sugar, cream cheese and a little lemon juice, until you have a buttery icing. Spread evenly on top of the cakes.

Gingerbread men

You will need:

Baking paper

14 oz (350 g) plain flour, plus extra
    for dusting

1 teaspoon bicarbonate of soda

2 teaspoons ground ginger

1 teaspoon mixed spice

5 oz (125 g) butter, chilled and cut
    into small pieces

7 oz (175 g) light soft brown sugar

2 tablespoons golden syrup

1 egg (beaten)

Gingerbread-man cutter

Decoration: currants, Smarties and icing pens

(Makes 8–12 depending on what size cutter you use)

1. Preheat the oven to 190 degrees C/gas 5 and line two baking sheets with baking paper.

2. Sift the flour into a bowl along with the bicarbonate of soda, ground ginger and mixed spice. Then rub in the butter until

it looks like crumbs. Now add the sugar, golden syrup and egg and stir it all together into a sticky dough. If it's too sticky, add a little more plain flour to the mix.

3. Roll out the dough on a well-floured surface until it is about ½ in (1 cm) thick. Cut out your gingerbread men then, using a spatula, slide them on to a baking sheet covered in baking paper.

4. Bake for about 15 minutes. When they are cool, use currants for eyes, icing pens to add a face and to stick Smarties on for buttons.

Things to Make and Do Indoors

She held up her crochet-work and said, "Look! I've crocheted nine whole rows and I haven't dropped a single stitch!"
Milly-Molly-Mandy Gets Locked In

Milly-Molly-Mandy is very good at turning old scraps of material and leftover wool into something special. If you'd like to do the same, it's a good idea to make yourself a craft box and start collecting useful bits and bobs: cardboard, wool, fabric, felt, old buttons and anything else that could come in handy. Then you'll be ready to have a go at some of Milly-Molly-Mandy's favourite crafts.

Patchwork

And over the teapot in front of Miss Muggins was a most beautiful cosy, all made of odd-shaped pieces of bright coloured silks and velvets, with loops of coloured cord on top. Milly-Molly-Mandy did like it!

Milly-Molly-Mandy Makes a Cosy

Patchwork is a clever way to turn old scraps of material into something special. The idea is to sew lots of different pieces of fabric together to create something completely new.

Before Milly-Molly-Mandy could make her patchwork tea cosy she had to find the bits of fabric. And that's probably the best part of patchwork – collecting lovely scraps of material.

Fabric shops often sell small offcuts, but it's much more fun to find your own. Why not start a ragbag of old unwanted material? It could be clothes that don't fit, faded cushion covers and curtains, torn party dresses, table cloths or old dressing-up clothes – anything at all really, so long as you like the look of it!

You can make all sorts of beautiful things from patchwork: aprons, shopping bags, quilts and, of course, tea cosies.

Learning to sew can take time. Ask a grown-up to help you get started and then put in lots of practice – it will be worth it because once you've learnt to sew you can make lots of lovely things.

"Oh Milly-Molly-Mandy!"said Mother, "what a – beautiful – cosy!"

And Mother was so pleased, and Milly-Molly-Mandy was so glad she was pleased, that they just had to hug and kiss each other very hard indeed.

Milly-Molly-Mandy Makes a Cosy

Little patchwork cushion

This is a great little cushion to get you started.

You will need:

4 small squares of fabric (whatever size you want – but 6-in (15-cm) squares work well)

A piece of fabric to be the back of your cushion (the same size as your four smaller squares added together, so about 12 in (30 cm) square

Needle and thread

Stuffing: old tights, cotton wool, old hankies, other fabric or wool

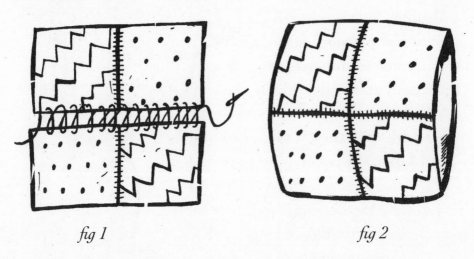

fig 1   *fig 2*

1. First thread your needle. This is a little bit fiddly but will get quicker once you get the hang of it. Tie a double knot in the end of your thread and you're ready to sew!

2. Start by placing two of your fabric squares with their patterned sides together. Sew along one edge (about ½ in/ 1 cm) so that when you open them out your two squares

form an oblong. Do the same thing with your other two squares. Ask an adult to iron them flat for you.

3. Now place your two oblongs with their patterned sides together and pin the long edge together on one side. It's a little bit bumpy as you go across the sewing you've done in the middle, but try to keep it neat!

4. Sew along this line, again about 1 cm from the edge of the fabric (*as fig 1*). Open out your material and you will have one big square! Ask an adult to iron this flat as well.

5. Now take your last fabric square, which will be the back of your cushion, and lay your patchwork on top of it so that the patterned sides are together. Pin and sew along three of the edges and half of the last edge, leaving a gap to stuff the filling into (*as fig 2*).

6. Stuff the cushion with whatever you've chosen to fill it with, then fold the edges in to make it look nice and neat and sew along the gap to finish it off.

Patchwork bag

You can use the same method to make a patchwork bag. All you do is leave the last seam open, then hem around the edges of the open seam to make them neat and stitch on ribbon handles.

Knitting

Then Milly-Molly-Mandy took one of the pennies to the little village shop, and bought a skein of beautiful rainbow wool.

"Grandma" she said, when she got home, "please will you teach me to knit a kettle-holder?"

So Grandma found some knitting-needles and showed Milly-Molly-Mandy how to knit. And though it had to be undone several times at first, Milly-Molly-Mandy really did knit quite a nice kettle-holder . . .

Milly-Molly-Mandy Spends a Penny

Knitting takes a bit of practice, but once you get the hang of it you can quickly create lots of useful things. The best way to learn is to watch someone else do it, so ask a grown-up to show you. If you find it too hard, don't worry; perhaps a grown-up could do the knitting for these projects, and you could do the decorating.

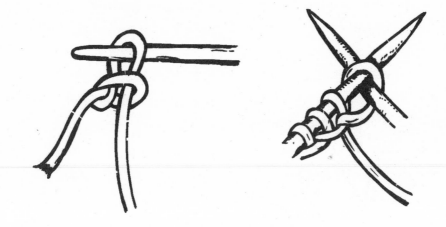

casting on

Finger-puppet friend

You will need:
A pair of knitting needles
A ball of wool
A needle to sew it together (a large tapestry needle is best)
Decoration for the face: glue, coloured wool, buttons, felt,
    tiny pompoms and anything else you can find!

1. Cast on 14 stitches. Knit 25 rows, until your knitting is approximately 4–6 in (10–15 cm) square, then cast off, leaving a 6-in (15-cm) tail of wool.
2. Fold your knitted square shape into a tube, then thread your needle on to the tail of wool and use it to sew your knitting together into a finger-puppet shape.
3. You can either glue or sew the face on to your puppet. You could use buttons for eyes, or stickers, or googly eyes. Try sewing on extra strands of wool for hair, or making your puppet a hat! You could make a funny person, a fairy or perhaps your favourite animal.

> ❀ ❀ ❀ **TIPS** ❀ ❀ ❀
> **Half-size needles are easier for**
> **small fingers to manoeuvre.**
> **Chunkier wool will make a thicker puppet,**
> **and you may need fewer rows.**
>

Knitted bookmark

This makes a lovely gift for anyone who likes to settle down with a good book. Use fine wool for this project, as chunky yarn would be far too thick to sit neatly between the pages of a book.

You will need:
A pair of knitting needles
A ball of wool
Beads (optional)

1. Cast on 8 stitches. Knit until the knitting is about 4 in (10 cm) long, then reduce both sides, by knitting two stitches together at the start and end of each row, until you are left with one remaining stitch. Cut the wool and thread it through the loop of this last stitch to tie off. Leave a tail on the end, for easy page-finding.
2. Try threading a few beads to the wool tail, knotting it at the end to secure them.

French knitting

French knitting is a bit like knitting and a bit like crochet – it's lots of fun and very easy to do. You can buy French knitting dollies in most toy shops, or make your own following the instructions below.

You will need:
A knitting dolly
Wool
A crochet hook

How to make your own knitting dolly:

❖ Tape four lolly sticks to the inside of a sweetie tube, open at both ends, so that they stick up about 1 in (2 cm) above the rim.

or

❖ Ask an adult to hammer four nails into the top of a wooden cotton reel.

1. Drop the end of your wool down the centre of the knitting dolly, so that approximately 4 in (10 cm) hangs out at the bottom.

2. Wind the wool twice around one of the spikes, in an anti-clockwise direction. Don't pull the wool too tightly (*as fig 1*).

3. Using the crochet hook, pick up the outsides edge of the bottom loop, lift it over the top loop, and let it drop into the centre of the dolly (*as fig 2*).

4. Now turn your dolly anti-clockwise so that an empty spike is towards you, and repeat the previous two steps, winding twice then lifting the bottom loop over the top loop. Continue until you have covered each spike.

5. Now go round again, but this time only wind the wool once around each spike before looping the bottom loop over the top loop. Carry on like this and eventually your knitting will appear from the bottom of your knitting dolly like a big long worm!

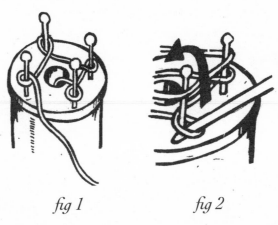

fig 1   *fig 2*

6. When your knitting is as long as you want it, lift it off the spikes, thread the end of your wool through the four loops left at the top and pull it tight. Tie a knot at the top to secure.

❀ ❀ ❀ **TIP** ❀ ❀ ❀

Your French knitting would make a lovely bracelet or necklace for a friend. You could add some beads to it to make it even more special.
If you want to change the colour of your wool, just tie a knot in the two ends and carry on knitting.

❀ ❀ ❀

Crochet

So Milly-Molly-Mandy sat in the middle of the floor and began crocheting. Crocheting is quite hard work when you've done only three and a half rows in all your life before, but Milly-Molly-Mandy crocheted and crocheted until she reached the end of the row; and then she turned round and crocheted and crocheted all the way back . . . and quite soon the bonnet was finished.

Milly-Molly-Mandy Gets Locked In

Basic crocheting is quick and easy to learn. All you need is a crochet hook, some wool and a bit of time to practise. Here's how to do it.

You will need:
Wool
A crochet hook

1. Ask a grown-up to make a slip knot on the crochet hook.
2. Hold the crochet hook in your right hand. With your left hand, wind the wool around the crochet hook, pull the wool down through the slip knot and you will create a chain stitch. (Don't pull it too tight, or you won't be able to get your loop and hook through the stitches.)
3. Keep repeating this process to make a longer chain.

4. If you want to stop here, cut the wool and loop it through your final stitch and knot it tightly.

5. If you want to carry on, you will need to start your next row.

6. With the last loop of your chain still on your hook, insert your hook into the back of the next loop along from the hook.

7. Bring the wool over the hook, like you did while making the chain, and pull it through the ridge. You will now have two loops on your hook.

8. Bring the wool over the hook again, and pull it through the two loops.

9. Repeat until you reach the end of the row.

10. To start the next row, turn your work around, pulling the row you just completed towards you. The hook will now be at the beginning of the work again.

11. Insert the hook under the two top loops of the stitch closest to your hook. Wind the wool over your hook as before, and draw the new loop through.

Very easy bracelet

You will need:
A crochet hook
Wool
Beads

1. Make a crochet chain that will fit your wrist (about 10–15 chain stitches). Tie it off at the end, but leave enough wool to thread on a few beads. Then tie up the two ends with a firm double knot.
2. Once you've got the hang of it, try crocheting a bracelet with two balls of wool at the same time, for a two-tone effect.

Create a crochet hair braid

You will need:

A crochet hook

Wool

Beads and feathers or ribbons to weave through

A hair slide or large kirby grip

1. Make a crochet chain the length of your hair. Tie off.
2. Thread a few beads on to the end and secure them with a double knot.
3. Attach the non-bead end of the chain to a hair slide or a hair grip by looping it on, or alternatively just pin the braid directly on to your hair by clipping it in place with the slide or grip.

Paper Projects

Little sailor dolls

Teacher drew a little sailor-girl, with a sailor collar and a sailor-hat and pleated skirt, on a folded piece of paper, and then she cut it out with Aunty's scissors. And when she unfolded the paper there was a whole row of little sailor-girls all holding hands.
Milly-Molly-Mandy Gets to Know Teacher

Paper-chain dolls are quick and easy to make. Try making sailor girls like Teacher, or design your own dolls. Dress them in sweetie paper skirts, with sequin sashes, or feather bonnets and fairy wings. Or try making them look like you and your friends. How about a different shape altogether? Instead of people, try making animals, insects, stars – or even robots!

You will need:
A long strip of paper, about 6 in (15 cm) wide – the longer it is, the more dolls you can make, so you could tape several pieces of paper together.
Pencils, crayons or pens
Sequins, scraps of fabric, sweetie wrappers, feathers, coloured paper
Glue

1. Fold the paper every 4 in (10 cm) or so, first one way and then the other, so that you have a concertina shape.
2. When you have finished folding the strip of paper, draw your doll shape on the front fold. Make sure your doll's hands reach right to the edge of the paper as this is where the chain of dolls will be joined.
3. Cut out your doll shape, but don't cut the sides where the hands touch.
4. Unfold your dolls and decorate.

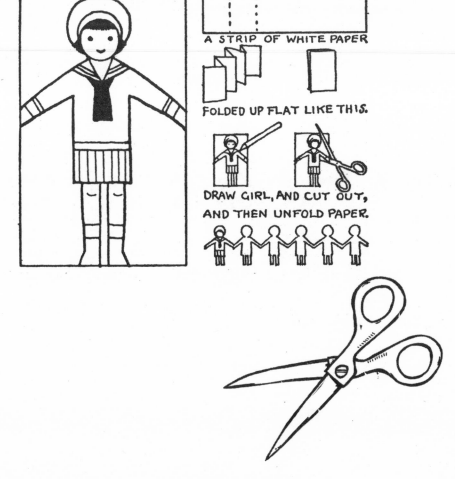

Make a dress-up doll

Another great way to play is to make your own dress-up doll. Use stiff cardboard for the doll, and make and change the clothes whenever you feel like it.

And when the lamps were lit Mrs Hooker brought out a beautiful paint-box and a fashion paper full of little girls, and Milly-Molly-Mandy and Milly-next-door each painted a little girl very carefully, and cut it out with Mrs Hooker's scissors, and gave it to each other for a keepsake.
Milly-Molly-Mandy Goes Visiting

You will need:
Tracing paper
Cardboard
Coloured tissue paper
Felt-tip pens
Small piece of Blu-tack
Decoration: sequins, ribbon, coloured paper

1. Trace over the doll and clothes opposite.
2. Fasten the tracing paper on to the cardboard and cut out the doll shape and clothes. Remove the tracing paper.
3. Draw a face and hair on your doll and decorate the clothes with pens, ribbons or sequins.
4. Use the Blu-tack to attach the clothes to your dolls.

❀ ❀ ❀ **TIP** ❀ ❀ ❀
**You could cut clothes out of magazines and stick them
on instead, or even cut them out of bits of fabric!**

Flat-family

Here's a quick way to make a doll's house. This is great for doing while you are on holiday.

You will need:

A large sheet of paper (or several
    smaller pieces sticky-taped
    together)
An old catalogue or old magazines
Scissors
A box to keep all your pictures in
    when you've finished playing

1. Draw a large house shape on your
    paper – start with a square, then
    draw a triangle roof, and finally
    divide your square into quarters, to make four rooms.
2. Now find your flat-family. Look through your catalogue and choose the people you want to live in your house. You might pick out a mum, a dad, a few children, grandparents and a pet or two. Cut them out – but make sure they are all about the same size, and that they'll fit in your house.
3. Next find furniture for your house. Cut out a bed, a kitchen, a sofa, a television – anything you like the look of! Then for the fun bit – fill your house with all your furniture and your paper people.

GRANDPA · GRANDMA · FATHER · MOTHER · UNCLE · AUNTY · MILLY-MOLLY-MANDY.

❀ ❀ ❀ TIP ❀ ❀ ❀

When you've finished playing, roll up your house, and store your people and furniture in a box ready for next time.

❀ ❀ ❀

Fairy fortunes

Will it rain on Saturday? Will there be cake for tea? Will your front tooth fall out before Christmas? Predicting the future is lots of fun. And here's a quick and easy way to do it: by making a fairy fortune-teller.

You will need:
A square of paper
A pen

1. Lay the square on the table in front of you. Fold it in half side to side and open it up again, then repeat by folding top to bottom. The creases now form a cross. Fold each corner into the middle and crease well (*as figs 1–5*).
2. Turn your paper over and fold the corners into the middle again (*as figs 6–8*).
3. Fold the whole thing in half, then push the thumb and forefinger of each hand under the outer flaps.
4. Now you should be able to move your fairy fortune-teller left and right and backwards and forwards (*as fig 9*).
5. Lay your fortune-teller flat again and write a number from 1 to 8 on each of the inner triangles.
6. Now lift each flap and write a different fortune underneath. They can be as silly as you like, for example:

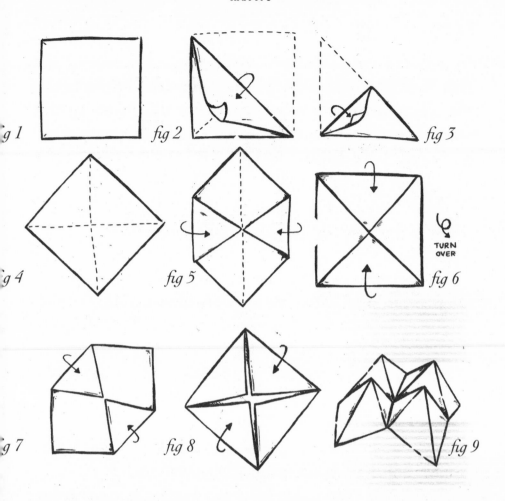

fig 1

fig 2

fig 3

fig 4

fig 5

fig 6 TURN OVER

fig 7

fig 8

fig 9

You will have a surprise on Saturday
Seven is your lucky number
You will be rich and famous
Beware of low-flying pigeons!

To tell someone's fortune, put your fingers and thumbs in the flaps and ask your friend to choose a colour. Then spell out the colour by opening and shutting the fortune-teller in alternative directions, once for every letter of the colour they have chosen. So, if they choose "red", move it three times:

R-E-D. Then ask them to pick a number, and again move the fortune-teller once for each number they have chosen. Then ask them to chose another number, but this time don't move the fortune-teller, instead lift the flap with that number on it, and read out your friend's fortune.

If you don't want to make a fortune teller, what about doing a **dare-picker**.

Make your dare-picker in the same way, but instead of fortunes, write funny dares under the triangles, such as:

Walk backwards with a book on your head
Hop on one leg for 2 minutes while singing a song
Do 100 star jumps with your tongue touching your nose!

The fortune-teller can also be turned into a cute little hand puppet.

Instead of colours and numbers, draw eyes on the outer triangles and colour the insides red, then cut out and stick a paper tongue inside the mouth of your puppet.

Instead of reading fortunes, you can make your puppet talk by putting your fingers and thumbs in the flaps.

Papier mâché

Papier mâché is very simple and you can use it to make all sorts of things. It's also nice and messy, so don't forget to put lots of newspaper down and wear old clothes!

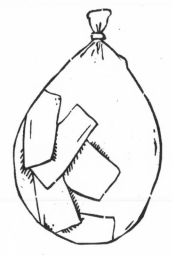

You will need:
Old newspapers, wrapping paper,
   magazines and sugar paper
A balloon
PVA glue, mixed with a little water
Paintbrushes
Acrylic paints

1. First tear your paper into tiny pieces.
2. Blow up your balloon and ask an adult to tie a knot in the end.
3. Brush some of your glue mixture on to the balloon and stick the bits of paper all over it, so that the edges overlap. When you have covered the whole balloon, hang it up to dry somewhere for about an hour.
4. When your first layer is dry, cover the balloon with another layer of paper scraps. Continue to add layers and let them dry until you have about six layers.
5. When your last layer is dry, pop the balloon using a pin or a needle. Pull the burst balloon out by its knot.

Hot-air balloon

You will need:
One papier-mâché-covered balloon
Acrylic paints
Paintbrushes
A small empty box or cardboard
    tube – or you can cut down a
    larger box to fit
String or ribbon
Sticky tape

1. Ask an adult to cut the bottom off your papier mâché balloon so that you have a nice neat edge.
2. Paint your balloon in lovely bright colours. Try stripes, spots and zigzags and make it really eye-catching! Then paint your box or tube to match, to make the basket.
3. When the paint is dry, use four equal lengths of string or ribbon to attach your basket to your balloon. Tape in place.
4. Now your hot-air balloon is ready to soar! You can hang it up by attaching a length of string to the top of the balloon. Why not let some of your favourite toys be passengers?

Fruit bowl

This is another way of using papier mâché, which is just as simple and just as messy!

You will need:
A plastic bowl
Petroleum jelly or cling film
Newspaper, old magazines or wrapping paper, torn into
  strips
PVA glue, mixed with water
A paintbrush

1. First, cover the inside of your bowl with a thin layer of petroleum jelly or cling film. This will stop the papier mâché from sticking to it.
2. Build up layers of paper as described on page 73. Make sure you go all the way to the edges – it doesn't matter if the paper overlaps the rim of the bowl.
3. Leave to dry completely, then remove the plastic bowl. Ask an adult to cut off any messy edges to create a nice neat rim.
4. Choose the paper you want to decorate your bowl with. You might like to use pictures torn out of old magazines, pretty wrapping paper or some coloured tissue. Start with the outside of your bowl, add one layer of paper and glue it in position. Fold the edges of this layer over into the bowl. Once this layer is dry do the same with the inside of the bowl. You shouldn't be able to see any newspaper at all when it's finished!

Wonderful Weaving

Paper weaving

You will need:
An A4 sheet of coloured paper
Old magazines
Scissors
Sticky tape

1. Fold your piece of coloured paper in half lengthways and draw lines on it, about 1 in (2.5 cm) apart, all the way along. Your lines should start at the folded edge and stop about 1 in (2.5 cm) away from the unfolded edge. Ask an adult to cut along these lines, then unfold the paper (*as fig 1*).
2. Tear out a few pages from your magazine, and cut them lengthways into long thin strips, approximately 1 in (3.5 cm) wide.

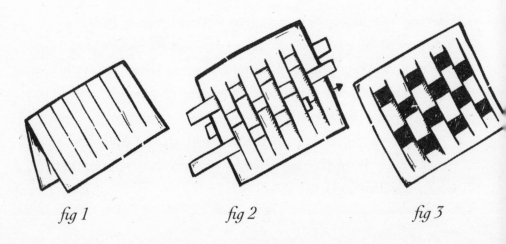

fig 1   fig 2   fig 3

3. Now take a strip and weave it over the first strip of your coloured paper, under the second, over the third and so on, until you reach the other side. Repeat with another strip, but this time weave it the opposite way to your last one – under the first strip, over the second, and so on. Carry on until you reach the bottom of your paper (*as fig 2*).

4. Fold the loose ends over to the back of your paper and tape in place (*as fig 3*).

5. There are lots of things you can make with your woven picture. You could stick a loop of string on the back to hang it up, or wrap it round an old pot or cardboard tube to make a pencil holder. (Secure the ends with double-sided or ordinary sticky tape.) Or try making a place mat or even a bookmark!

Fabric weaving

You will need:
A sheet of stiff cardboard, about 8 x 12 in (20 x 30 cm)
Different coloured ribbons
Fabric, cut into long strips

1. Ask an adult to cut an even number of slits in the short ends of your cardboard, about ½ in (1 cm) apart.
2. Slip the end of your ribbon into the first slit and tape in place at the back of the card. Now wind the ribbon round the card, threading it through each slit as you go, round and round from front to back. Tape the end of the ribbon in place.
3. Tie your strips of fabric together so that you have one long length, and weave them through the ribbon strips in the same way as you did with paper weaving, above.
4. When you get to the bottom of the card, tie the end of your fabric in a knot round the ribbon.
5. Turn the cardboard over and cut through the ribbon, then carefully remove your weaving from the cardboard.
6. Knot the ribbon ends together in pairs, then trim them all to the same length.

Decorate Old Frames

A great way to reuse old unwanted things is to decorate an old photo frame. (Make sure you ask a grown-up for permission first though!)

Cardboard frames that come with school and nursery photos are particularly easy to transform. Decorate them with sparkly plastic jewels, sequins or feathers. Try to customize the frame to suit the person you want to give it to; old stamps, newspaper cuttings, Lego bricks, ribbons, bows, silver stars or even jelly beans and dolly mixtures can really brighten up and personalize an old frame.

D. Hammett, Photos.

Melon-seed Necklace

Here's a fun way to make a
pretty necklace or bracelet
for someone special.
The seeds look a bit like
shells, but they're much
easier to make holes in for
threading.

You will need:

A melon
Fine elastic thread – or ordinary sewing thread
Sewing needle
A few beads

How to make

1. First, cut open the melon and scrape out the seeds. Rinse
   well, then put them on kitchen paper and dry them out
   for a few days. (You could put them next to a radiator to
   speed this up.)

2. Thread your needle and knot the end. If you are using
   elastic thread, you can make the necklace a little bit shorter,
   as it will stretch over the wearer's head. If you're using
   ordinary thread, make sure it's long enough to fit easily
   over the head.

3. Thread the seeds by piercing a hole in them with the
   needle. They should still be soft enough to thread easily –
   but be careful, as needles are sharp! If you find this a bit

fiddly, ask a grown-up for help.

4. If you have any beads, thread them on too. You can make any pattern you like. When you've threaded enough seeds and/or beads, just knot the ends together.

❀ ❀ ❀ **TIP** ❀ ❀ ❀
You can use any sort of seeds for a necklace like this – try sunflower seeds, pumpkin seeds, watermelon seeds or apple pips.
❀ ❀ ❀

There are lots of household things that you can thread on a string to make a pretty necklace.

❖ Dried pasta shapes are easy to thread. Colour them in with felt-tip pens before you start threading.

❖ Try using coloured drinking straws. Chop them into shorter lengths and then thread them on to your string.

❖ You can also make your own beads with foil – just scrunch it into lots of little balls of the same size, then push a needle and thread through the centre of each one.

Puppets

When it's dreary outside, a puppet show is the ideal way to raise everyone's spirits. Choose your favourite story to perform and choose one of the methods below to make the stars of the show!

Sock puppets

Here's a great way to use up odd socks!

You will need:
An odd sock (make sure it's definitely an odd sock; not just one whose partner has got lost in the laundry basket)
A needle and thread
Buttons for eyes
Felt or fabric for the mouth
Glue
Scraps of wool for hair
Pipe cleaner

1. Pull the sock on to your hand, putting your thumb in the heel and your fingers in the toe. When you touch your thumb to your fingers, you will see your puppet's mouth!

2. Sew buttons on to the sock for eyes – around where your knuckles are when the sock is on your hand. If you don't have buttons, you could cut out felt circles and stick them on instead.

3. Cut an oval of felt and glue it to the sock where your puppet's mouth is – you could also add teeth and a tongue at this stage.

4. Scraps of wool glued or stitched on make great hair – or even a mane for a horse or a lion.

5. Try using a pipe cleaner for antennae, or to shape into a pair of glasses.

Shadow puppets

You will need:
Pencil
Scissors
Thin black card
Split pins
Wooden kebab sticks
Sticky tape
A large sheet
An anglepoise lamp

1. Draw the head, body, legs and arms of your character separately on to the black card.
2. Cut out each piece carefully and lay them all out on the table. Now cut the arms and legs in half where elbows and knees would be.
3. Fasten all the pieces together by overlapping them and pushing the split pins through the card, folding them back on the other side. Now your puppet has moving joints!
4. Tape the wooden kebab sticks to the back of your puppet – one along its back, one on each hand and one on each foot. You won't be able to move all of them at once, but it's good to have as much movement as possible.
5. Your puppets can be as simple or as

complicated as you like. You could make a simple tree shape, or a spider with eight moving legs.

6. Hang your sheet up somewhere and shine the lamp directly at it from behind. Hold your puppets up between the lamp and the sheet and your audience will see their shadows moving. Try to keep out of the way of the light yourself though, or they will see yours too!

Sew a Pretty Purse

Milly-Molly-Mandy is always thinking of clever ways to earn extra pocket money. But where does she keep her pennies? Perhaps in a purse just like this . . .

You will need:
A piece of coloured felt about 6 in (15 cm) square
Pencil
Needle and threat
A small scrap of coloured wool
A button
Decorations, if you have them

1. Draw a large rectangle on your felt, with one curved end. You could draw round a jar or other round object to get a nice even curve. Your shape should be about 4 in (10 cm) long and 2½ in (6 cm) wide (*as fig 1*).
2. Cut out this shape and lay it flat on the table. If your material is patterned, then make sure the pattern is facing up. Fold the square end of your fabric up towards the curved end, so that it stops just before the curve starts. Pin and sew the sides together (*as fig 2*).

3. Now turn your material inside out so that the patterned side is on the outside and your stitches are hidden. Fold the curved end down so that you have an envelope shape.

4. To make a fastener, sew a button on to your purse, then make a loop out of wool and fit it over the button. Sew the ends of the loop on to the back of the curved end of the purse, so that you can close your purse by looping the wool around the button (*as fig 3*).

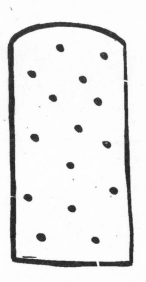

fig 1

5. Sew or glue on some sequins to make your purse look extra pretty.

❖ As well as being a perfect place to keep your pennies, you could also use this purse when you lose a tooth. Put the tooth in the purse, and leave it under your pillow at bedtime, so that the tooth fairy can swap it for a coin.

fig 2

fig 3

Little-friend-Susan's Plaited Friendship Bracelet

Milly-Molly-Mandy spent her penny on a big yellow sugar-stick for Little-friend-Susan, who broke it carefully in two, and gave her half.
Milly-Molly-Mandy Enjoys a Visit

Here's a lovely present to give a special friend. It's easy to make, and fun to do. Invite a friend to play and make one bracelet each, then swap them and wear them every time you play together.

You will need:
Three different coloured balls of wool
Sticky tape
Beads

1. Cut 2 lengths of each colour of wool, each about 12–16 in (30–40 cm) long. Knot them together at one end, making your knot about 3–4 in (8–10 cm) from the top.
2. Now tape the ends to a table so that they're held securely.
3. Separate the wool lengths by colour and start to plait them together. Do this by lifting A and moving it into the middle, then repeating with B and C. Repeat, right then left, right then left, pulling the wool tightly as you go, until

88

you've plaited a bracelet that is long enough to fit round your wrist, with a bit to spare. When the bracelet is long enough, knot tightly, to hold the plait together. Then cut the wool lengths, leaving about 3 in (8–10 cm) loose.

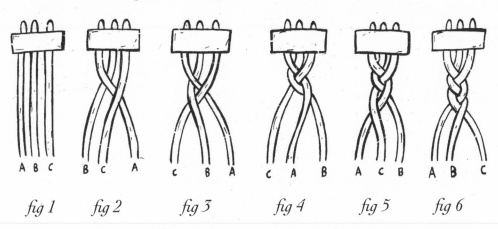

A B C   B C A   C B A   C A B   A C B   A B C

fig 1   *fig 2*   *fig 3*   *fig 4*   *fig 5*   *fig 6*

4. Now plait the loose ends at the top and bottom of your bracelet, but this time don't double up the wool lengths – plait them singly instead. Divide them into two separate sections of 3 wool ends each, and make two small braids to tidy the ends. Bind the ends neatly together with small scraps of wool, and trim. Finally, tie the bracelet on to your friend's wrist.

5. If you like, you can add beads to make the bracelet even more colourful. Thread them on to the wool as you plait it – or if they are larger beads, you may be able to thread them on to the bracelet when you've finished plaiting.

A more complicated friendship bracelet

This type of bracelet is a bit harder to master, but once you have the basic technique you can quickly make beautiful bracelets for all your friends.

You will need:

Two lengths each of three different coloured wools or
    embroidery threads – three times longer than you want
    your finished bracelet to be.

A safety pin

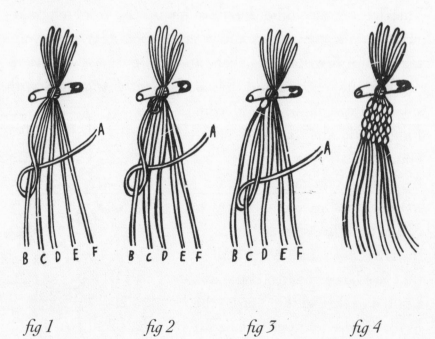

fig 1   fig 2   fig 3   fig 4

1. Knot all the threads together about 2½ in (6 cm) from the top and push the safety pin through the knot. Attach the safety pin to a cushion (ask permission from an adult first) and put it on your lap.

2. Hold thread B taut with your left hand, and with your right hand take thread A and knot it around thread B twice (*as figs 1 and 2*). Now do the same thing with threads C, D, E and F, until thread A is all the way at the other side (*as fig 3*).

3. Now repeat this with thread B, knotting it twice over each of the other threads until it reaches the other side. Carry on doing this with each thread and you will start to see stripes appear. There's no limit to how many threads you start with – the more you use the wider your bracelet will be! (*as fig 4*)

4. When your bracelet is the right length, tie the ends in a knot, leaving enough thread to fasten the ends together round your wrist (or your friend's).

Write a Letter

"I do wish the postman would bring me a letter sometimes," said Milly-Molly-Mandy coming slowly back into the kitchen. **"He never does . . ."**
"If you want the postman to bring you letters you'll have to write them to other people first," said Mother.
Milly-Molly-Mandy Writes Letters

Nothing can quite match the thrill of receiving a letter. But as Milly-Molly-Mandy's mother wisely points out, you're far more likely to get a letter if you write one to someone first.

Choosing who to write to is important. An older person can be a good choice – perhaps a favourite aunt or uncle or a grandparent. You could write to a friend who lives far away; not only will they have more news to tell you because you see them less often, but it can be fun to find out about a different part of the country – or, even better, another country altogether!

You will need:
Paper
Pens or pencils
An envelope
Stamps

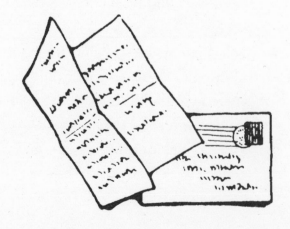

It's always more fun to write a letter on nice paper. Ask a grown-up if you can borrow their stationery. Parents often have nice notelets, writing paper or special postcards tucked away somewhere. If not, make your own!

Find an ordinary sheet of paper and make it look special by decorating it with drawings or stickers. Try pencilling in margins down the sides of the paper and use that space to draw pictures in, then write your letter in the middle.

If a large sheet of paper feels like too much to fill, cut it in half, and use smaller pieces. Alternatively, divide a large sheet in two, draw a picture on one half and write the letter underneath. Perhaps your picture might illustrate what you're writing about.

Sometimes it's hard to write in straight lines, so you could use a ruler to pencil faint lines across the space you're going to write in. You can use the lines to guide your writing and then rub them out afterwards.

Thinking of things to write about can be hard. So here are a few ideas:

❖ Tell your friend about what you've been doing at school – what books you're reading or films you've seen.

❖ Tell them about what's growing in your garden, or about a favourite pet or hobby. You might like to tell them about a baking or craft project you've made – you could even send them your favourite recipe!

❖ You can ask questions too – and when your friend replies they'll be able to answer them.

❖ Write about things you're planning to do, places you're

hoping to visit or places you've been to recently.

❖ If you know any good jokes, you can put them in too.

❖ If your friend lives far away, you can tell them all about your town. You could even draw a picture or a map of the town, and mark on all your favourite places: the best cafe, your favourite shop or a good place to feed the ducks.

Before you seal your envelope, find something light and flat to put in with the letter – perhaps a postcard of your town or some stickers, or a bookmark or a finger puppet you have made. If you have any photographs of yourself, why not tuck one inside too?

Then write your friend's address on the envelope, stick on the stamp and post it.

Milly-Molly-Mandy does like letter-writing, because now she has got three more friends!
Milly-Molly-Mandy Writes Letters

Have a Party

"Susan," said Milly-Molly-Mandy, "I've got a plan (only it's a great secret). I want to give a party in our barn to Farver and Muvver and Grandpa and Grandma and Uncle and Aunty . . ."
Milly-Molly-Mandy Gives a Party

You don't need a birthday to throw a party. Sometimes it's just fun to have one for no reason whatsoever. Invite a few friends, or family – or even just your favourite toys. Party hats get everyone in the right mood, and they're very easy to make.

Perfect party hats

Robin Hood hat

You will need:

A large rectangular sheet of
   paper (newspaper is good, or
   stick three sheets of A4 paper
   together along their long sides).

Sticky tape

Felt-tip pens

Decoration: stickers, feathers,
   tissue paper

fig 1

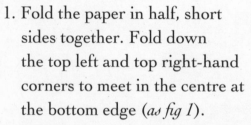

fig 2

1. Fold the paper in half, short
   sides together. Fold down
   the top left and top right-hand
   corners to meet in the centre at
   the bottom edge (*as fig 1*).
2. Fold the bottom edges up on both
   sides and crease well (*as fig 2*).

3. Now decorate! Use pens or
   crayons to colour your hat in, or
   you could even paint it.

Crowns

These are simple to make, and you can decorate them to suit your party. Try making shiny jewel crowns, mermaid tiaras or sparkly fairy crowns.

You will need:
A long strip of cardboard
Tissue paper
Decoration – plastic jewels, sequins, cotton wool, kitchen foil
Glue
Sticky tape
A dinner plate

1. Cut a zigzag down the middle of your strip of cardboard – this will make two crowns (*as fig 1*).
2. Next, wrap one of the strips round your head to get the size right, then sticky tape the ends together.
3. Now decide what sort of crown you are making. If it's for a king or a queen, make a tissue paper insert by drawing round a dinner plate on tissue paper, cutting it out and sticking it inside the rim of the crown. Plump it up to create a crown effect. Then stick cotton wool balls along the bottom edge of the crown, and finish off with jewels.
4. To make a mermaid's tiara, cut out silver foil fish, starfish and shell shapes. Colour your

fig 1

crown blue like the sea, then stick on your foil shapes. You could also make a seaweed tissue-paper fringe to attach to the back of your crown.

5. Fairy crowns can be made in much the same way, but decorate with sparkly glitter and sequins. Try making your own fairy jewels to stick on your crown by dipping small balls of cotton wool into runny glue, then rolling them in glitter.

6. Don't forget to make a fairy wand too. Cut out two thick cardboard star shapes, stick them together and cover in foil. Decorate with glitter, then sticky-tape the star on to the top of a long pencil or a sturdy twig from the garden wrapped in tinfoil.

Party bunting

Brighten up your party room with this quick and easy bunting.

You will need:
Coloured paper
Cardboard
Pens
String
Glue
Blu-tack

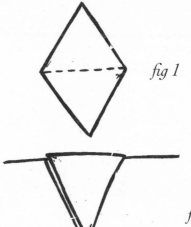

fig 1

fig 2

1. Ask a grown-up to draw and cut out a cardboard diamond shape for you. This will be your bunting template. It can be any size you want.
2. Next, use the template to draw 20 diamonds on different coloured paper (or use white paper and colour the shapes in).
3. Cut out your diamonds. Then fold them in half to make triangle shapes (*as fig 1*).
4. Now decorate the shapes to suit the theme of your party – use glitter or sequins, cut out foil shapes, or just draw on shiny patterns.
5. Next, stretch out a length of string, and drape the bunting flags over it. Then glue or staple the two sides of the bunting flags together (*as fig 2*).

Things to Make and Do Outdoors

It really was the most beautiful fresh morning, full of little bird-voices . . . And Milly-Molly-Mandy with the breeze in her hair, ran hoppity-skip down to the brook through the long grass and dewdrops that sparkled all colours in the sun . . .
Milly-Molly-Mandy Gets Up Early

Milly-Molly Mandy likes nothing better than being outdoors, whether it's fishing trips with Billy Blunt, building a den or blackberrying with Little-friend-Susan. You can have all sorts of adventures outdoors, even if you don't have a garden.

Make a Den

**And at five o'clock that very afternoon Milly-
Molly-Mandy and Little-friend-Susan and Billy
Blunt were sitting drinking milk from three little
mugs and eating slices of bread and jam and
gingerbread from three little plates, and feeling
just as excited and comfortable and happy as ever
they could be, up in the Milly-Molly-Mandy nest.**
Milly-Molly-Mandy Finds a Nest

Making an outdoor den has to be one of the best ways to
spend an afternoon. It doesn't have to be a tree house like
Milly-Molly-Mandy's (though if you've got a big tree in your
garden, some planks of wood and a grown-up to help, there's
no reason why you can't make one). It's just as much fun to
make a garden den and it can be as simple or fancy as you like.

Simple dens

**They tried with an old counterpane, which Mother
had given them, and two kitchen chairs; and they
managed to rig up quite a good tent by laying
the poles across the chair-backs and draping the
counterpane over. They fastened down the spread
out sides with stones; and the ends, where the
chairs were, they hung with sacks. And there they
had a perfectly good tent, really quite big enough
for two – so long as the two were small, and didn't
mind being a bit crowded!**
Milly-Molly-Mandy Camps Out

1. Find a big bush with space behind it. As
   long as there's enough room for you,
   and perhaps a few toys and a snack,
   then it can be your den.
2. If you happen to have a tree in
   your garden, you could make a
   very quick den by draping a
   cotton sheet or a large piece
   of tarpaulin over a few of
   the low-lying branches.
   Secure with clothes
   pegs, and weigh down
   the bottom edges with
   sticks or rocks.
3. If you're short of
   bushes or trees, you

can make a perfectly good den by using two garden chairs with a blanket slung across them. (Be sure to weigh down the chairs to prevent tipping. Piles of books or magazines work well.) Then weigh down the edges of the blanket with stones.

4. If you've got a slide in your garden, you could use the space underneath it for a den. Cover with a sheet, and peg in place with clothes pegs. And if you're lucky enough to have a big slide with a wooden platform on the top, you've pretty much already got a tree house. Just cover the platform and you can create your own den in minutes.

5. If the tent is large enough and your parents don't mind, you could even spend a night in it. Falling asleep under the stars on a summer's evening is a special experience to treasure.

Decorate your den

Once you've built your den, make it cosy with a few cushions (best to ask first), books or magazines, pens and paper and a few toys. A notepad and binoculars are good too, so that you can spot and record all the wildlife you see.

You could also decorate your den with flowers and leaves, inside and out.

Why not turn your den into a secret clubhouse? Invite your friends, and play detective games or spies.

You could simply enjoy your den by yourself. Lie back, close your eyes and listen to all the garden noises: insects, birds, the wind in the trees. A good game is to try to count the different noises you can hear. You'll be amazed at how easy it is to separate noises when you close your eyes and concentrate.

And of course the best bit about a garden den is that you don't need to travel too far for a snack. Why not have a mini-picnic in your den? Fruit and muffins are a tasty treat with little mess. Don't forget to take a water bottle too – den building can be thirsty work.

Daring dens

Garden dens are great, but building a den in the woods can be really exciting – especially if you do it with friends. Some forestry groups like the Woodland Trust even run den-building activities at weekends.

To make a woodland den, find a big tree with a wide trunk

to be your back wall. Then scour the wood for fallen branches and foliage. Drag the branches back to your tree, then prop the larger ones up against it, using smaller branches and twigs to weave in between the gaps.

Once you've made your den, it's the perfect place to watch the woodland wildlife. Look out for birds, rabbits and squirrels. And don't forget to look down too; the forest floor is the perfect place to discover unusual insects. Keep a notebook, or draw a spotting sheet, and write down or draw everything you see.

And then the little bunny turned his head and ran skitter-skutter along the ditch and up the bank, into the wood and was gone.
Milly-Molly-Mandy Goes Blackberrying

Look out for signs of shyer animals. Try to find their tracks in the mud: deer, badgers, fox, birds . . . You could even try making a print of the tracks you find. To do this you will need plaster of Paris (which you can find in a craft shop), and a strip of stiff cardboard or flexible plastic.

❖ Make a ring with your card or plastic and secure it with tape. Place the ring around the track and push it into the earth slightly so that the plaster doesn't seep out from underneath it.

❖ Mix up your plaster (you will need to take a small bowl and water with you), pour it gently over the track, then wait for it to set.

❖ If you don't want to make a plaster cast, just try drawing the print instead.

❀ ❀ ❀ **TIP** ❀ ❀ ❀

You may also be lucky enough to spot an owl dropping. They're quite fascinating; inside you'll quite possibly find the tiny skeletons of their last meal – small woodland creatures like mice and voles.

❀ ❀ ❀

Woodland World

**Father led the way to where some big, old
trees were stooping round as if trying to hide
something. And in behind them Milly-Molly-
Mandy and Little-friend-Susan and Billy Blunt
saw a deep round hole in a wet rock which was
simply covered over with beautiful green ferns and
moss. And water, sparkling like crystal and cold
as ice, was dripping down into it over the mossy
rocks at the back.**
Milly-Molly-Mandy Goes for a Picnic

There's always something special to do or see in a forest,
whatever the season. And if you visit regularly you'll be amazed
at how much the woods will change from month to month.

Trees

You can tell the difference between types of tree in lots of ways. Here are a few to start with.

Oak

You can spot an oak tree by its leaves, which have wavy edges, and by its acorns. If you find acorns on the ground, there will be an oak tree nearby.

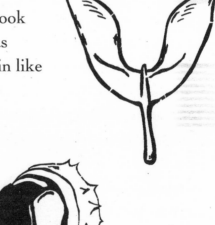

Sycamore

The seeds of Sycamore trees look like little pairs of wings, and as they fall from the tree they spin like helicopter blades.

Horse chestnut

You might know the horse chestnut as a conker tree! Conkers start appearing in the autumn – the best time to collect them is at the beginning of October.

Pine

You'll recognize a pine tree by the scent of
its leaves – they smell like Christmas! You
might also see pine cones on the ground
surrounding the tree. These are worth
collecting as you can make lots of things
with them.

Cherry

Cherry trees have beautiful pink or white
flowers in spring, and lots of fruit in summer.
It's best not to eat cherries unless you know
that they are an edible variety – most aren't.

**. . . then they set to work filling their
empty pockets with acorns and conkers.
But Milly-Molly-Mandy collected pine-cones,
because Father and Mother and Grandma and
Grandpa and Uncle and Aunty did like a pine-cone
fire . . .**

Milly-Molly-Mandy Goes for a Picnic

❀ ❀ ❀ **TIP** ❀ ❀ ❀

**Forests often have nature trails to follow, with bird
or squirrel spotting places marked. Some even have
stone sculptures dotted among the trees. Many forests
also have special activities on offer like bat spotting,
badger watching, pond dipping and campfire building.**

110

Blackberrying

**. . . Milly-Molly-Mandy and Little-friend
Susan set out with big baskets (to hold the
blackberries) and hooked sticks (to
pull the brambles nearer) and stout
boots (to keep the prickles off) and old
frocks (lest the thorns should catch).**
Milly-Molly-Mandy Goes Blackberrying

Fruit always tastes best when you've just picked it yourself.
Blackberries are particularly brilliant, because so often
they're free! One minute you can be out enjoying a lovely
country walk and then quite by chance you stumble on a
giant hedgerow full of them.

Milly-Molly-Mandy is an experienced picker. Not only
does she know the best places to find them, she also knows
what equipment you need:

❖ A basket (or pot) to put them in
❖ A hooked stick to pull them down (useful if you're
  short)
❖ Stout boots to keep the prickles off (beware; the
  prickles can be very sharp)
❖ And old clothes in case they get torn (. . . or stained
  from the juice)

Ask grown-ups where to find the best berry patches. Some of
the best places are known to only a few people, who return

to them each year, so it's worth doing your homework to find out where to go.

There are lots of great recipes to make with blackberries (see the cookery section for some ideas). But sometimes the best bit is just picking and tasting, especially when the berries are still warm from the sun.

❀ ❀ ❀ **TIP** ❀ ❀ ❀
Try to only eat berries that are too high up for dogs to reach (in case they have gone to the toilet on them), and don't eat too many in one go or you could end up with tummy ache.
❀ ❀ ❀

Weather Watching

Learning about the weather is not only good fun but a great way to get closer to nature. Start off by making a simple chart that just shows what the weather is like where you live, then move on to making your own mini weather station in your garden!

Simple weather chart

Draw different weather pictures around the edge of a paper plate such as a sun, a rain cloud, a tree blowing in the wind, a snowman . . . Then cut out a long arrow-shaped pointer from card or paper. Make a small hole in the centre of your plate. Fix on your pointer with a paper fastener, and then move it around to point out the day's weather. Sticky-tape a string loop on the back of the plate and hang it near a window.

To make your chart more interesting, why not add a smaller circle inside your paper plate with the seasons marked on it. Add another, shorter pointer, and you can show the weather and the season at the same time.

Here is the weather

You could also have a go at making your own weather forecast and even present it to your family and friends, as though you are on television.

You will need:
A large sheet of paper
A smaller sheet of paper
Pens and paper
Cardboard
Blu-tack

1. First, draw a map on the large sheet of paper. It could show the whole country or just your area.
2. Next, draw weather pictures on the smaller sheet. These might include a sun, a storm cloud, raindrops, mist, hail, snow – or you could make up your own symbols, for example a pair of wellies for rain, an ice cream for sunshine . . .
3. When you've finished, cut the pictures out and stick Blu-tack on the back so that you will be able to add them to your map as you do your forecast.
4. Now find somewhere to hang your map – perhaps on the back of a door or in your bedroom. Then stand in front of it and give your weather forecast.
   It doesn't need to be real – just make it up!

Rain-catcher

Find out how much rain falls each day by making a rain catcher.

You will need:
A plastic bottle with the top cut off
A ruler
Permanent marker
A plant pot and gravel to stand it in

1. Using the ruler, mark your bottle in inches or centimetres from the bottom to the top.
2. Next, find a good place in your garden to put it (not too sheltered, as you'll get less rain).
3. Stand your rain-catcher in the plant pot with a shallow layer of gravel round the bottom. This will prevent it from being blown over.
4. Then wait. You can check your rain-catcher every day to find out how much rain is falling. If you like, you could even make a simple chart to record the week's rainfall. (When you've finished with the water, use it to water any plants.)

Cloud Watching

Lying back on a patch of grass and watching the clouds is a lovely way to enjoy nature. See what shapes you can see: a teapot, a face, a teddy bear . . .

Now look more closely and see if you can spot these cloud types:

❖ Cirrus – the high white wispy ones

❖ Stratus – long layers of cloud that cover the sky

❖ Cumulus – white puffy clouds with fluffy tops

❖ Nimbus – rain clouds

When you spend time watching clouds, you'll notice they travel at different speeds and heights. Clouds can tell you which way the wind is blowing and what the weather will be. The darker the cloud, the more rain inside it!

Cloud pictures

You can recreate all the different sorts of clouds you see in the sky with cotton wool. Sketch what you see in a notebook first so you get them exactly right!

You will need:
A sheet of blue paper, or white paper painted blue – the
    bigger the better!
A stick of glue
Cotton wool balls

1. Draw your cloud shapes on the paper first, then go over your lines with glue.
2. Tear, stretch and fluff your cotton wool to make the right shapes and textures for your clouds, then stick them to the paper. You could even label them – cirrus, nimbus, stratus and cumulo-nimbus!

Watch the Stars

Stargazing is just as much fun as cloud watching. You don't need to know anything about stars to enjoy them. Just wait for a good clear night, then wrap up warm and head for the garden. Take a flask, a blanket and binoculars if you have them.

To get a really good view of the starry sky, you need to be in pitch darkness – away from streetlights and houses. A camping trip is ideal, especially if you're deep in the countryside with nothing else around.

With a bit of help, you should be able to pick out some familiar star patterns. These are a bit like signposts that can lead you to other stars.

Start by finding the Plough (also known as the Big Dipper), which looks like a long-handled pan. Then see if you can spot the North Star, which is close by. This is the star that sailors have used for centuries as a way to navigate across the seas. Now see if you can find Orion and Orion's Belt: the three stars across the middle of Orion.

The Internet is a good place to find more information about stars and you can print off star charts that show you where to look and what to look for. You might also find news

The Ploug

Orion

on special events to watch out for, like meteor showers.

Also consider joining your local astronomy club. If you go along to one of their meetings, you'll probably be able to have a look at the stars through a telescope – a breathtaking sight. If you get the chance, also look at the moon – if you're lucky, you'll be able to see the craters on its surface.

Make a lucky star

These little stars are very quick and easy to make once you know how. You can give them to your friends so that they can make a wish – who knows, it might come true! You could even write a short message, wish or secret on the back of the paper before you fold it.

You will need:

Strips of paper, about ½ in (1 cm) wide and 12 in (30 cm) long. Origami paper works well, or wrapping paper – card will be too thick

1. Start by tying a loose knot in the strip of paper towards the end. If you are using a paper with a pattern only on one side of the paper, be sure the pattern is facing towards the outside of the knot (*as fig 1*).
2. Pull on the paper strip gently to tighten the knot. Then gently flatten it to form a pentagon shape.
3. Fold the short end of the paper to one side of the knot, and tuck into the knot so that it is hidden (*as fig 2*).
4. Taking the long end of the paper strip, fold around the pentagon knot shape an edge at a time, creasing gently as

you fold. Don't press down on the creases too hard – just enough to hold the shape. Keep going until you only have a short end left (*as fig 3 and 4*).

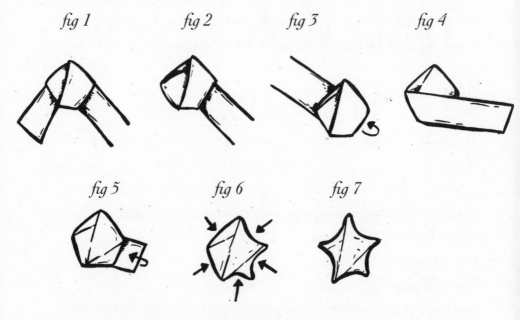

fig 1 fig 2 fig 3 fig 4

fig 5 fig 6 fig 7

5. Tuck the short end into the pentagon shape, trimming if necessary to make sure the end doesn't show (*as fig 5*).

6. Hold the pentagon shape in one hand and use one of the fingernails on your other hand to gently press one of the flat edges so that it bends inwards in the middle (*as fig 6*). Do this for all of the flat sides. You might have to practise this technique until you get it perfect, but when you do you'll have a star shape! (*as fig 7*)

Things to Make and Do in the Garden

But, somehow, nothing ever tasted quite so good as the things which grew in Milly-Molly-Mandy's own little garden!

There wasn't much room in it, of course, so she could grow only small things, like radishes, or spring onions, or lettuces . . .

Milly-Molly-Mandy and the Surprise Plant

Having a garden of your very own is a magical experience, even if it's just a miniature garden planted in a bucket. Learning how to care for plants isn't just fun, it's useful too – as Milly-Molly-Mandy discovered when she grew a pumpkin. And, even if you don't have a garden, there are lots of things you can grow indoors. Here are some good ideas to keep little green fingers busy.

Make a Miniature Garden

"I wonder," said Milly-Molly-Mandy, "If I shall grow a little garden in a bowl, and send it to the flower show!"
Milly-Molly-Mandy Makes a Garden

As Milly-Molly Mandy discovers, making a miniature garden is very exciting (and actually very simple to do).

You will need:
A container
Soil
A trowel
Plants

1. First, you need something to plant your garden in. Milly-Molly-Mandy uses a brown pottery-pie dish for hers, but any container would do: an old kitchen basin, a planting trough, a bucket, a basket – even an old wheelbarrow.
2. Next, put some small pebbles in the bottom of your container to help with drainage.
3. Then add the soil. You can dig up some soil out of your own garden (ask first), but potting compost would work best as it's full of goodness to help your plants grow.
4. Now, the fun part: choosing what to put in your garden.

**. . . Milly-Molly-Mandy set the first
plant in her garden. It was a tiny
little holly-tree which she had found
growing almost in the path under
the big holly-tree by the hedge . . .
Next she went poking about down
by the brook, and she found some
nice moss-grown bits of rotten wood . . . and then
she planted some grass and a daisy root in the rest
of the space, and it really looked quite a pretty
garden.**

Milly-Molly-Mandy Makes a Garden

Just like Milly-Molly-Mandy, if you look around your back garden, you're bound to find lots of little plants that have grown from fallen seeds. The best place to look is underneath big trees such as oaks and sycamores. When you find a plant you like, carefully use your trowel to dig around it, taking care not to damage the roots, gently remove it, then make a hole in your container garden and replant it, filling the soil in around the plant and pressing down firmly.

Also look out for interesting rocks, grasses, moss or pieces of bark that would look nice in among your plants.

As well as using plants from your garden, you could save your pocket money and buy some from your local garden centre. There you'll find lots of small plants, which are ideal for a miniature garden. Look out for the ones with tiny flowers such as lobelia, alyssum, nasturtium, pinks and violas.

To make your garden more interesting, you could add a small gravel path between the plants, using tiny stones, or push an upturned jar lid into the soil, and fill it with water to make a pond. If you have a doll's house, you could borrow a table and a few chairs for garden furniture – and perhaps a doll to sit in your garden.

If you're not interested in dolls, you could make a dinosaur garden by adding a few plastic dinosaurs to peep out from between the plants. Little fern plants look perfect in a prehistoric garden.

When your garden is finished, don't forget to water it. You will need to keep it well watered – but not too much.

It looked so real you almost felt as if you could live in the little green cave, and go clambering on the rocks, or climb the tree, if you wished!
Milly-Molly-Mandy Makes a Garden

Once you've made one miniature garden, why not make another – perhaps a rockery garden with small alpine plants, or a cactus garden with several different cacti planted in a mixture of sand, gravel and soil. Or try a herb garden, which smells (and tastes) lovely, with plants such as rosemary, thyme, mint or lavender.

Miniature gardens are a good way to learn about plants and how to care for them. Perhaps later you could have your own corner of the garden and grow some plants from seed.

Bird Watching

Grandma was round by the back door, sprinkling crumbs for the birds (as it was just their busy time with all the hungry baby-birds hatching out).
Milly-Molly-Mandy Gets Locked In

Bird watching can be very exciting as you never know what you might see. The best way to start is by putting food out for the birds. This is particularly essential in winter, when birds often struggle to find enough food. You can buy wild bird seed in pet shops or garden centres. There are lots of different types, depending on what sort and size of bird you're hoping to attract.

You don't need a fancy bird table to feed the birds – you can hang food from tree branches, lay it on top of an upturned plant pot or sprinkle it along the top of a fence (though beware of cats, who often stalk birds while they are eating). And don't forget fresh water. A shallow dish of water, tucked securely into the branches of a tree, is ideal.

String peanut feeder

She saw a nest on a branch with a little bird peeping out of it.

"It's all right, Mrs Bird," said Milly-Molly-Mandy. "I won't frighten you."
Milly-Molly-Mandy Gets Up a Tree

Peanuts are a great source of fat for birds and a very quick treat to make is a monkey nut string, which you hang from a tree.

You will need:
String
Monkey nuts
Large blunt tapestry needle (or you could make holes with a knitting needle)

1. Thread your needle with the string, and tie a knot in the end. Then thread the monkey nuts on to the string by piercing a hole in them.

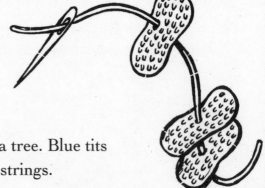

2. Tie another knot in the top, then hang from a tree. Blue tits particularly love peanut strings.

Other ideas:

❖ Half a coconut, rinsed and hung from a branch
❖ Mild grated cheese (very popular with robins and wrens)
❖ Uncooked porridge oats
❖ Toast crumbs – ask an adult if they will turn the toaster upside down for you!

Binoculars are useful, but not essential. You'll be amazed at how much birdlife you'll spot just by sitting still and watching for a while. Keep a journal and write down or draw the birds you see. You could include details of what they eat, and how often they visit your garden.

To learn to recognize birds, have a look in the library for a good bird-spotting book or visit the RSPB's website. It has lots of useful information to get you started, and also details of some special places you can visit to watch rare birds – including peregrine falcons and unusual water birds. Sometimes there are even special dens at these places called hides where bird watchers can sit, out of sight of the birds, to get a closer view.

Grow a Pumpkin

". . . It's a pumpkin! Oh-h-h!" said Milly-Molly-Mandy. Fancy! – a real pumpkin, like what Cinderella went to the ball in drawn by mice, growing in Milly-Molly-Mandy's own little garden!
Milly-Molly-Mandy and the Surprise Plant

Even though she only has a tiny patch of garden, Milly-Molly-Mandy manages to grow radishes, spring onions, lettuce . . . and a large pumpkin! This is how to do it.

You will need:
Pumpkin seeds
Small plant pots (or yogurt pots with holes in the bottom)
Compost
Space in the garden for the pumpkin to grow
Straw

1. The best time to plant your pumpkin seeds will depend on the type and size of pumpkin you're growing – so check the back of the seed packet for advice. Generally you sow pumpkin seeds in April, and the fruit will be ready to pick in the autumn.
2. Start by planting one seed in each small pot. (Even if you just want one pumpkin, it's best to plant a few seeds just in case some don't grow.)

3. The seedlings should start appearing within two or three weeks. Keep them inside if you can, in case of late frosts. When the roots poke through the bottom of the pot, transfer them into bigger pots.

4. Once the risk of frost has passed and your plants are bigger put them in the garden, but make sure they'll have space to grow. (The back of your seed packet will tell you how big they will be, and how much room they'll need for their leaves.)

5. To plant out your pumpkin, dig a hole and fill it with compost and manure. Overfill the hole to make a mound shape, then make a hole in it and plant your seedling. Press down firmly and water every day. You could use some plant food too, if you have it.

6. After about six weeks your plants will grow yellow flowers which will eventually turn into pumpkins. You only want two or three flowers on each plant, so pinch out the others.

7. When the pumpkins appear, put some straw underneath to stop them from spoiling. Also watch out for (and remove) slugs and snails, as they will eat your pumpkin.

8. When the pumpkin is fully grown, ask a grown-up to cut it off the plant. The stalk will be quite thick and tough, and they will need to use a sharp knife.

There are all sorts of delicious things you can make with your pumpkin. If you are using yours as a Halloween lantern, then you can still use the insides to make pumpkin soup or pie – and don't forget to save the seeds to plant next year.

❀ ❀ ❀ TIP ❀ ❀ ❀
Find out how to make pumpkin soup on page 19.
❀ ❀ ❀

Make a Mini Scarecrow

This scarecrow isn't scary enough to frighten any birds, but it's quick and fun to make and will brighten up a little garden.

You will need:
An old wooden spoon
A permanent marker
A piece of fabric
A large elastic band
A long pipe cleaner
A yogurt pot

1. First, make the face by drawing on the wooden spoon with your permanent marker.
2. Then wrap the fabric around the spoon and secure it with the elastic band.
3. Add the pipe cleaner, twisting it around the elastic band to make the arms. Bend the ends into loops for hands. You could add more fabric for sleeves if you want – again secure with elastic bands.
4. Now add a yogurt pot hat, and your mini scarecrow is ready to go in the garden!

131

Make a Grass Head

"That's all right," said the Blacksmith. "I always notice things grow best for people who get muddy noses."
Milly-Molly-Mandy and the Surprise Plant

This is a fun indoor gardening activity – a funny-faced creature that in a week or two will grow its own hair.

You will need:
A pair of old tights (or stockings)
Grass seed
Sawdust
An elastic band
Small elastic band
A yogurt pot
Googly eyes or a permanent marker
Glue

1. Cut the foot part off one leg of the tights and fill the end of the toe with grass seed. Now stuff the foot with sawdust until it is a ball shape. Tie the end tightly and secure with the elastic band.

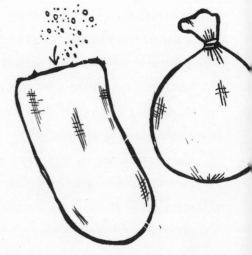

2. To make a nose, pull part of the tights into a small round shape at the front of your head, and secure it using a small elastic band.
3. Now put your grass head into the yogurt pot, and make a face on it using googly eyes or a permanent marker pen.
4. Water it, and in a week or two your funny face will grow a mop of hair, which you can cut or style.

Cress head

> **She watered it every day, and shaded it if the sun were too hot; and at last the little seeds grew into a lovely clump of fresh green mustard-and-cress, that made you quite long for some bread-and-butter to eat it with.**
> *Milly-Molly-Mandy Spends a Penny*

This little fellow is a bit like a grass head, but you can eat its hair! Cress tastes delicious in salads or on egg sandwiches.

You will need:
A yogurt pot (or an egg carton section)
Cardboard and pens or paint
Cotton wool
Mustard and cress seeds

1. First, decorate your yogurt pot. You can do this by wrapping cardboard around it, and colouring it with pens or stickers. A face works well, so that when the cress grows it will look like hair.

2. Next, fill the pot with cotton wool. Add water to make it nice and damp, then carefully sprinkle cress seeds on to the cotton wool. Leave it on a sunny windowsill, making sure the cotton wool stays damp. The seeds should start to sprout in a day or two – and after about a week you will have enough cress to eat!

❀❀❀ **TIP** ❀❀❀

**You could even grow your name in cress!
To do this, line a tray with several layers of
damp kitchen roll, then carefully sprinkle the
cress seeds to spell out your name or initials.**

❀❀❀

Create a Wormery

Presently Mr Moggs scratched out a worm along with a tuft of dandelion, and Milly-Molly-Mandy squeaked because she nearly took hold of it without noticing (only she just didn't).

"Don't you like worms?" asked Mr Moggs.

Milly-Molly-Mandy and Dum-Dum

Worms are a gardener's best friend. They mix up the soil and turn old leaves and other garden waste into good stuff our plants need to grow strong and healthy. By making your own wormery, you'll be able to see exactly how they do it.

❀ ❀ ❀ **TIP** ❀ ❀ ❀

Don't forget to put the worms back in the garden when you've finished studying them.

❀ ❀ ❀

You will need:
A see-through container
Sand and soil
A trowel
Old fallen leaves
Black paper
2 or 3 worms

1. First, find a see-through container. You could use an old plastic fish tank, or a large jar, or even a big plastic bottle with the top cut off.

2. Fill your container with layers of soil and sand, one after the other – each about 1 in (2.5 cm) deep. Finish with a thicker layer of soil, and then spread some old leaves and vegetable peelings on top. Add a small amount of water – worms like it damp, but not too wet, and definitely not dry. (If it's too dry, they may die.)

3. Now go outside and dig up some worms. A good trick is to use your watering can to moisten the soil, as this brings them to the surface. Two or three worms will be enough. Have a good look at them, but be careful not to hurt them, then add them to the wormery. Watch as they burrow downwards, away from the light.

4. Next, cover the top of your container with a lid, or cling film with air holes punched through. Wrap your container in black paper and leave it somewhere dark and cool for a week. When you take the paper off, you will see how the worms have mixed up the soil and taken some of the leaves down to eat.

Bug Watch

Searching for mini-beasts is not only fun, it's also a good way to learn about the interesting world of insects. All you need are your eyes (though if you have a magnifying glass and any books about bugs, they'll be useful too).

Check under rocks and old rotting wood. Peer into bushes and grass and underneath flowerpots. If you've got a sandpit, look under that too. Anywhere dark and damp will usually contain interesting insects. Why not make a note of what you see – or create a bug journal with pictures and facts about your favourite insects? Look out for spiders, beetles, ants, woodlice, centipedes and earwigs.

A good way to attract bugs is to leave a small piece of food in the garden overnight – try half an orange, or perhaps a slice of melon. When you go back to it in the morning, you'll probably find slugs, snails or ants around it.

You could also make your own mini nature pond. Plastic sandpits work well for this. Tip out the sand (ask first), and pour a small amount of water into it. Leave it for a few weeks, and you'll be amazed at the insects that will set up home there – especially if you position it under a tree. If you don't have a sandpit, a shallow basin would work just as well.

137

Frog Pond

One place was just full of tadpoles – they caught ever so many with their hands and put them in the jam-jars, and watched them swim about and wiggle their little black tails and open and shut their little black mouths.

Milly-Molly-Mandy Goes on an Expedition

Frogs are another friend to the gardener. They eat the pests that attack our plants, so it's a good idea to encourage them into the garden.

To make a pond, dig a hole in a shady corner of the garden, ideally in a place that's a bit untidy with plenty of old leaves, rocks and pieces of wood – the sort of places where frogs can hide. You may need a grown-up to help you with this.

You could line the hole with a plastic pond shell, which you can buy from a garden centre, or you could use a plastic sandpit, or a watertight plastic liner secured with rocks.

There are plenty of frog-friendly pond plants available from garden centres, but you could also allow the grasses and existing plants to grow naturally around the edges of your pond. Also put in some flattish rocks – especially around the edges – so that the frogs can get out easily.

Now wait patiently, and your pond should eventually attract frogs to your garden. If you're lucky, the frogs will lay eggs there, and you'll be able to see their fascinating life cycle, from frogspawn to tadpoles to froglets to frogs!

Grow Bean Shoots

This is another gardening activity that can be done indoors. All you need is a glass jar and a few beans.

You will need:
A jar
Beans or chickpeas (if you're using dried beans, soak them for half an hour first)
Kitchen roll

1. Scrunch up a few sheets of kitchen roll and stuff them inside the jar. Then push a bean down the side of the jar, between the glass and the kitchen roll. Do the same with another bean on the other side of the jar. (You may have space for three beans if your jar is large enough.)

2. Pour a little water into the jar, to soak the kitchen roll. You will need to keep the kitchen roll damp by watering it every day. Put your jar on the windowsill, in the sunshine, and in a couple of weeks your beans will have grown into shoots.

3. When they're large enough, you could pot them up and grow them in the garden. If they get very tall you may need

a stick to support them – push it into the earth next to the plant and tie it loosely to the stalk with some string or twine.

This is a fun activity to do with family or friends. You could even hold a competition to see who has the tallest shoot after two weeks.

Super Sunflowers

These hardy flowers not only look pretty, they're also easy to grow. Look out for different varieties – dwarf sunflowers or giant ones that will grow taller than you.

You will need:
Sunflower seeds
A big pot or a sunny patch of garden
Canes and string
Compost
Trowel

1. You can plant sunflower seeds in pots or in the garden. If you want to grow your flower in a pot, try one of the smaller varieties, as sunflowers need plenty of room to grow.

2. If you're growing your plants in the garden, find a sunny place – make sure it's quite sheltered as strong winds may snap your sunflowers when they grow taller.

3. Dig some small holes, plant one seed in each and cover them with compost. Water the seeds daily and after two or three weeks the seedlings will appear. As they grow bigger, support them with canes – tie your sunflowers loosely to the canes with string.

4. Make sure you keep watering them – sunflowers are thirsty plants. Eventually they will start to flower. Don't forget to measure how large they grow!

5. When the sunflowers have finished, collect the seeds that are in the middle of the flower heads and keep them in an envelope ready for next year. You could even make your own paper seed packets and pass them on to friends.

6. Sunflower-growing competitions are great fun. Get everyone involved, then write their names on lolly sticks and push them into the soil next to each person's seed and see whose plant grows the tallest. Perhaps you could make a sunflower-shaped medal for the winner!

Games for a Sunny Day

These traditional garden games are ideal to play with larger groups of friends. If you haven't got a big enough garden, the park would work just as well. Why not try making your own silver foil medals to hand out to the winners at the end? Don't forget refreshments – outdoor games are thirsty work, so have a tray of drinks at the ready!

After that they tied their ankles together – Billy Blunt's left and Milly-Molly-Mandy's right – with Billy Blunt's scarf and practised running with three legs across the field. It was such fun, and Milly-Molly-Mandy shouted with laughter sometimes because they just couldn't help falling over.
Milly-Molly-Mandy Goes to a Fête

Three-legged Race

**Then they entered for the three-legged . . . A man
tied their ankles, and shouted "Go!" and off they
all started, and everybody laughed, and couples
kept stumbling and tumbling round, but Milly-
Molly-Mandy and Billy Blunt careered steadily
along till they reached the winning-post!**
Milly-Molly-Mandy Goes to a Fête

The secret of this game is teamwork: learning to move at the
same pace, speed and stride as your friend. (It's much easier
if they are roughly the same size as you!)

To begin, stand side by side in pairs, then use a soft scarf
to tie your inside ankles together – making your four legs into
three! Put your arms around one another's shoulders to give
you more balance, and then you're ready to go. Now make
your way from one end of the garden to the other, as fast as
you can. The fastest couple are the winners!

Egg-and-spoon Race

It's probably best not to try this with a real egg (unless it's been hard-boiled first), because until you get the hang of it, you'll probably drop the egg rather a lot, which could be messy!

Start off with a large tablespoon and something to balance on it. Pretend wooden eggs are ideal. Small bean bags work well or try a golf ball. A tennis ball would be fine too – so long as your spoon is big enough to hold it.

Now, holding your "egg" and spoon in one hand, put your other hand behind your back and set off as fast as you can – heading for the end of the course.

If you drop your egg, you must stop and pick it up before continuing. The winner is the first person to get to the end.

You can make the game more exciting by putting out obstacles to go around. Try using cones to weave in and out of (if you haven't got cones, you could use old milk cartons, or plastic bottles with marbles or rice inside to weight them down). You could also use hula hoops to step inside like giant stepping stones. Or you could even try playing the game blindfolded!

Another variation of this game is "balloon on the tray", where you fill a balloon with water and try to run with it on a small tray all the way to the end of the course.

Beanbag Balance Game

Here's a good way to test your balance. The idea of the game is to get from one end of your course to the other with the beanbag on your head, as fast as possible, without touching it or dropping it. The winner is the first person to reach the end of the course, but the faster you go, the more chance you have of dropping the beanbag! You can make the game harder by adding some obstacles to your course.

If you haven't got beanbags, you could make your own. All you need to do is sew two pieces of sturdy fabric together and fill them with small dried beans, lentils or sand. It's a good idea to put your filling inside another bag – an inner bag – so that there's less chance of it leaking. To do this, sew the inner bag first, and then sew your outer bag around it.

If you haven't got time to sew a beanbag, you could make a quick one by filling a sealable sandwich bag with the filling. (Be sure to squeeze all the air out before you seal it.) Put it inside two further sandwich bags to prevent leaking. Finally, secure the edges with masking tape. This bag won't last as long as the fabric one, and it might be a bit slippery – but it should be fine for a few turns!

Wheelbarrow Race

This is another game where teamwork is the key to success. It is played in pairs with one person being the wheelbarrow and the other person the pusher. The wheelbarrow person has to walk on their hands, supported by the pusher who holds on to their ankles. They have to walk (or, even better, run) the length of the course. The winners are the first pair to make it to the finishing line.

❀ ❀ ❀ TIP ❀ ❀ ❀
If you're the wheelbarrow person, be sure to tuck your top into your shorts, otherwise it'll fall over your face and you won't be able to see where you are going!
❀ ❀ ❀

147

Garden Obstacle Course

The best thing about this game is that you can design the course however you like – with as many obstacles as you want. You can also use elements from other games such as the egg-and-spoon race and beanbag-balance as part of your course.

The idea is to get from one end of the garden to the other as fast as possible, climbing over, under or along a variety of obstacles. You can also include a few stop-offs where you have to do a challenge in order to carry on along the course.

Here are some ideas:

- ❖ Old planks to walk along
- ❖ Cushion stepping-stones to jump along
- ❖ Balance a beanbag on your head and drop it into a basket
- ❖ A net, old blanket or piece of tarpaulin pegged down, to scramble under
- ❖ A tunnel to crawl through
- ❖ Hula-hoop jumping
- ❖ Dribble a ball around cones (or old milk cartons/plastic bottles)
- ❖ Throw a number of small balls into a box
- ❖ Egg and spoon section
- ❖ Water balloon on the tray
- ❖ Sack race section: use an old sack or pillowcase, get inside it, then jump!
- ❖ Do ten star jumps and twenty hops on the spot!

Games for a Rainy Day

Once upon a time, one morning, when Milly-Molly-Mandy went off to school, it was raining and raining.

"Oh, what a nasty wet, rainy day!" said Little-friend-Susan, running out to join her.

Milly-Molly-Mandy and a Wet Day

Even when it's raining Milly-Molly-Mandy always finds some-thing fun to do. Here are some good ideas to keep you busy too.

Funny-people Paper Game

Then the games began, and they were fun! They had a spoon and potato race, and musical chairs, and putting the tail on the donkey blindfold, and all sorts of guessing games.
Milly-Molly-Mandy Goes to a Party

This is a great game to play with friends – perfect for a rainy day. The idea is to make lots of funny-looking people by each drawing part of a person, then passing the drawings on for the next person to add a bit more. Here's how to play.

You will need:
A sheet of paper, cut into strips
A pencil

1. Sit at the table and give everyone a pencil and a strip of paper.
2. Everyone starts by drawing a head with a neck at the top of their strip of paper. It can be any sort of head you like – perhaps with crazy hair, or a funny nose, or amazing spectacles. Or it could be a character like a pirate, a mermaid or even an alien! Whatever you draw, the most important thing is not to show your picture to anyone – and don't look at anyone else's picture either.
3. When you have all finished drawing a head and neck,

fold the paper down so that only the bottom of the neck is visible.

4. Now everyone passes the picture to the person on their left so that you all have a new strip of paper. Don't be tempted to unfold the head. (If you look, it won't work!)

5. Now everyone draws a body down to the waist, with arms and hands. When you've all finished, fold the paper down, this time leaving only the bottom of the waist visible. Again, you mustn't show anyone or look at other people's drawings.

6. Pass the drawings on. This time, with your new bit of paper, draw the legs, right down to the ankles – no feet yet though.

7. Again, fold the paper over so only the bottoms of the ankles are showing, then pass it on.

8. Now add feet. They could be big hairy yeti feet, or perhaps some dainty little ballerina shoes!

9. Fold, and pass your strip on again. Now everyone unfolds their person and you all show each other the crazy people you've created! Whose picture is the funniest?

10. You could colour the drawings in, cut them out and make a funny picture with them.

Memory-tray Game

You and your friends can test your memory with this simple tray game.

Ask a grown-up to make up a tray in secret with lots of different everyday objects on it.

For example there could be a pencil, an apple, a sharpener, a sweet, a pair of scissors, a roll of sticky tape, a carrot, a key, a bar of soap, a cotton reel, a toothbrush, a feather, a clothes peg, a coin, a paper clip, a pebble, a pot plant, a golf ball, an onion – anything they can find really. They mustn't show you yet and they should cover the items with a tea towel until you are ready to start.

The tray is then uncovered and you have one or two minutes to memorize as many of the things on it as you can before it is taken away.

When the tray has gone, you must each write down as many of the things as you can remember. The winner is the person who remembers the most items.

Billy Blunt's Fun Fishing Game

So they fished and they fished along the banks, and sometimes they saw quite big fish, two or three inches long, and Billy Blunt got quite excited and borrowed Milly-Molly-Mandy's net; and they got a number of fish in their jam jars.
Milly-Molly-Mandy Goes on an Expedition

You don't need a riverbank to make and play this fun fishing game with your friends, just some bits and bobs and a magnet! Here's what to do:

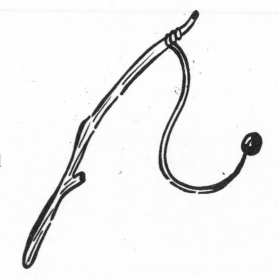

You will need:
Paper
Scissors
Paper clips
String
A stick, or a long cardboard
    tube – the kind you get
    inside a roll of wrapping
    paper is ideal)
Pens

1. Cut out simple fish shapes from your sheet of paper. Give each one a number – the numbers will be the points you get if you catch that fish.
2. Fasten a paper clip to the nose of each fish.

3. Next make your fishing rod. Attach a piece of string to the end of the cardboard tube or sturdy twig from the garden – this will be your fishing line. Then tie a magnet to the end of the fishing line. If you don't have a proper magnet, you could use a fridge magnet instead.

4. Now you are ready to fish! The best place to do this is behind the sofa.

5. Drop all your fish on to the floor behind the sofa, then take turns to lean over with the fishing rod and try to catch as many as you can in a certain time.

6. The person who gets the most points in that time is the winner.

Flap the Fish

This is another fun fishy game using large tissue-paper fish.

You will need:
Tissue paper
A large paperback picture book to
  waft your fish!

1. This is very simple. All you need
   to do is cut out large fish shapes
   from the tissue paper – one for
   each person playing.
2. The object of the game is to "flap"
   your fish, by fanning it with your
   book, from one end of the room to
   the other.
3. The winner is the first person to
   get there.

Blow-ball Obstacle Course

This is a fun game to play on the kitchen or dining room table.

You will need:
Straws
Kitchen foil
Obstacles such as salt and pepper pots, sharpeners, rubbers, etc.

1. First of all make your ball by rolling up some kitchen foil. If you want the game to be harder, make a bigger, heavier ball. Smaller foil balls are easier to move around the table.
2. Next, set up your obstacle course. You can use anything you like for this – salt and pepper pots, rubbers, rulers, packets from the larder – anything you can find. You can make obstacles to go through (like goal posts), or obstacles to go around, like a cup, or even obstacles to go up, like cardboard tubes.
3. Once you've set your course, take your straw and blow your foil ball around it. If you're playing with friends you could time each other and see who gets around the course in the fastest time.

Knock the Box!

This game is a bit like a fairground coconut shy! It's a great way to use up old boxes.

1. Ask a grown-up to save empty packets for you. Stock-cube boxes, gravy granule cardboard tubes, cereal packets and rice boxes all work really well. So do old milk containers, but rinse them out first.
2. To weigh your boxes down and make them harder to knock over, you could put a few marbles or a lump of plasticine inside them. Next give each one a number. This will be the number of points you'll get if you knock it down!
3. Now line them up on the kitchen table, or on the back of the sofa, and find a soft ball or a beanbag to throw at them.
4. Stand back and have a go – see how many you can knock down in a minute.
5. The same boxes can also be used for indoor skittles. Just line them up on the floor and roll a ball to knock them down!

Shake, Rattle and Roll!

**They stood in a row, and Billy Blunt lifted his
shovel and poker violin, and Milly-Molly-Mandy
her comb-and-tissue-paper mouth-organ, and
Little-friend-Susan her saucepan-lid clappers;
and they played and sang, hummed and clashed,
Happy Birthday to You!**
Milly-Molly-Mandy and the Golden Wedding

A fun rainy day game is to make your
own band. Have a good rummage in
your toy box to see what you can find,
and then add to your instruments with
these easy home-made ones. Invite your
friends to join your band.

Rice shakers

You will need:
A container with a lid
Sticky tape
Rice, beans, lentils, popping corn, pasta or dried peas
Coloured paper, pens, stickers for decorating

1. Find an old container with a lid; you could use an old plastic
   bottle, or a gravy granules cardboard tube, or a small crisp

tube, or maybe a stock-cube box.

2. Pour in some rice, lentils, popping corn or dried peas, then seal the container with sticky tape.

3. Now wrap the coloured paper round your shaker, secure with sticky tape and decorate with felt-tip pens and stickers.

4. You could make lots of different sized shakers and change the sounds they make by putting different things inside them or different amounts.

Pan-lid cymbals

Borrow two small metal pan lids with handles, and you've instantly got a set of cymbals.

J.L.B.

Drums

Make a great drum out of a metal tin with a plastic lid – empty baby-milk or coffee canisters are ideal. Cover with wrapping paper and decorate. Use an old wooden spoon or chopsticks for drumsticks.

Tissue-box guitar

String an empty tissue box with four or five rubber bands to make a guitar and strum or pluck them where they pass over the opening. Different widths of rubber band will make different sounds.

Cardboard tooter

Turn a cardboard tube into a tooter by covering one end with a circle of baking paper, and securing it with a rubber band. Sing or hum into the other end.

Bottle xylophone

Ask an adult to find you some empty glass bottles, and fill each one with a different amount of water. If you hit the bottles gently with a teaspoon, they will each make a different note! If you adjust the amount of water in each bottle carefully, you will be able to play tunes.

Dressing Up

"Let's both dress up and be ladies," said Milly-Molly-Mandy.

"Ooh, yes, let's," said Little-friend-Susan.

Milly-Molly-Mandy and Little-friend-Susan looked awfully funny – especially when they tried to put on the things which Milly-Molly-Mandy had outgrown. They laughed and laughed. (The attic was rather a nice place for laughing in – it sort of echoed.)

Milly-Molly-Mandy Dresses Up

Dressing up is an excellent way to spend the day when the rain means you can't go outside. If you're lucky, your parents or older brothers and sisters won't mind you trying some of their clothes on, but if they'd rather you didn't there are lots of costumes you can make from things in the house. Here are a few ideas.

Pirate costume

Wear plain shorts and a stripy T-shirt. Make an eye patch out of some black card and some string or elastic, and tie a piece of red material

around your head for a bandanna. Ask if you can borrow an eyeliner pencil to draw a big curly moustache!

Fairy costume

Wear pale colours and anything sparkly you can find. Make a wand by sticking a cardboard star to the end of a wooden spoon – wrap ribbon around the handle to make it extra pretty. Cut some wing shapes out of card and use glitter to give them some fairy sparkle! Attach them using string or ribbon.

Robot costume

Collect some different sized cardboard boxes – one big enough for your body, one for your head, and four smaller ones for your arms and legs. Paint them silver or grey, and stick bottle tops on for buttons and dials. Draw a face on your head box and cut out eyeholes.

Black cat costume

Put on black trousers or leggings and a black top. Stuff a black stocking or one leg cut from a pair of black tights with some old newspaper, and pin it to your waistband at the back. Make yourself some ears by sticking two triangle shapes to a hairband, and ask a grown-up to draw some whiskers on your face with eyeliner pencil.

Tablecloth Town

All you need for this game is a paper tablecloth and some pens or pencils. It's a great way to have some quiet time during a children's party, or just a fun way to while away a wet afternoon.

The idea is to create your own town by drawing on a plain white paper tablecloth.

Think of all the things you'd like to have in the town: a park, a duck pond, a cafe with tables outside, a school, a playground, a river, houses, shops, a hill, fields with animals, a city farm, office blocks, a castle, a garden centre, a fire station, people walking their dogs – anything you like. Then create your town!

If you're doing this with friends, each take a different side of the town to draw, and then meet in the middle.

This would make a great keepsake to remember a special birthday party. When you've finished your town, ask your friends to sign their names, then put it away for safe keeping. When you're much older, you can take it out again and remember the great party when you made it.

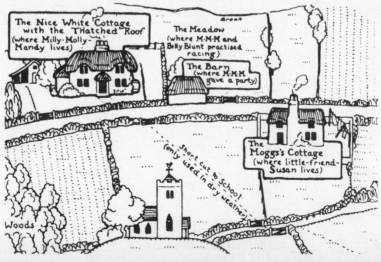

Catch Cup

You can make this fun toy in minutes. The object of the game is to catch the ball in the cup. See how many times you can catch it without missing.

You will need:
A paper or plastic party drinks cup
String
Foil
Sticky tape

1. Wrap your foil around the end of the string and scrunch it into a tight ball with the string inside.
2. Now sticky-tape the other end of the string to the inside of the cup – you may need to fiddle around with the length of the string until it feels right, but about 10–12 in (25–30 cm) should be about right.
3. All you have to do now is flick the ball up and try to catch it in your cup.

Tiddlywinks

This is a great game to play with old buttons. You can use any shape or size, though tiny ones are a bit more difficult.

All you need is a cup or bowl to "tiddle" into and the buttons to "wink" with.

The object of the game is to use one button to flip the others into the cup. To do this, you press your button down on the edge of another, and it will flip forwards (or backwards sometimes).

Once you've got the hang of it, you'll be able to control how far the button jumps.

Try to "wink" as many of the buttons into the cup as you can in one minute.

Button Box

If you haven't got any old buttons, why not start a button box? Look around the house and you'll probably find a few – sometimes down the side of the sofa, or in a kitchen drawer, or in a sewing box maybe (watch out for needles).

Ask a grown-up if they've got any old buttons, look out for them in jumble sales and junk shops, or cut them off old clothes.

You'll be amazed at how many different types and shapes and sizes of button there are.

As well as being great for tiddlywinks, you can make amazing patterns on the floor with buttons. Try making a face shape, or a fish, or a rainbow, or just a long line of buttons like tiny stepping stones.

They make great counters for board games. (You could even invent your own board game!)

Use them as money when you're playing shop, or stick them on socks to make a sock puppet's eyes.

They also make a great noise if you rattle them – use them as shakers to make music.

Make a Flick Book

The pictures were lovely! There was a very nice man who rescued a lady just in time (Milly-Molly-Mandy knew he would), and there was a funny man who ran about a lot and fell into a dustbin . . .
Milly-Molly-Mandy Goes to the Pictures

Make your own mini animation in minutes by drawing a flick book. Here's how.

You will need:

A small notebook (or lots of small sheets of paper or card carefully stapled together)

A pencil (and rubber, in case you need to change the picture)

To make a flick book, all you need to do is draw a simple story on the pages of the notebook. Then, when you flick the pages of your notebook, it will look as if your pictures are moving.

The trick is to keep it simple, so you might just draw a dancing stick man, or perhaps a little chick hatching from an egg, or a flower growing from a seed – or even just a face changing expression, from smiley to sad and back again.

Whatever you draw you need to be able to draw it again and again (about thirty times), with just a tiny change each time. Lined paper can help with this, so that you make your picture the same size each time.

A dancing stick man is a good one to start with.

Start at the back of your notebook. Draw a stick man at the corner of the page. On the next page trace over the stick man but change him slightly – perhaps raise one of his legs or change the position of one arm.

Then turn to the next page and repeat the same picture, but again with a slight difference – perhaps one arm will be up, the other arm down.

Change the picture slightly on each page; you could have him do the splits, or stand on one leg, or jump in the air, or turn over on to his head! Keep going until you have drawn on about thirty pages.

When you flick the pages of your notebook, your man should look as if he is dancing.

Things to Make and Do in the Spring

And then one day she came home after school a bit later than usual, because she and Little-friend-Susan had been picking wild-flowers and primroses under a hedge, very excited to think that spring had really come.

Milly-Molly-Mandy Writes Letters

There are lambs in the fields, chicks are hatching and the first green shoots are appearing through the ground. Spring has arrived and with Easter fast approaching there are lots of fun activities to enjoy.

Make an Easter Tree

This is a simple way to brighten up a room. All you need is a fallen branch or some twigs from the garden.

You will need:
A small branch or twigs
A plant pot, big enough to support your tree
Gravel, sand or small pebbles
Bright ribbons
Eggs to decorate your tree (papier mâché, foil, felt or
  chocolate)

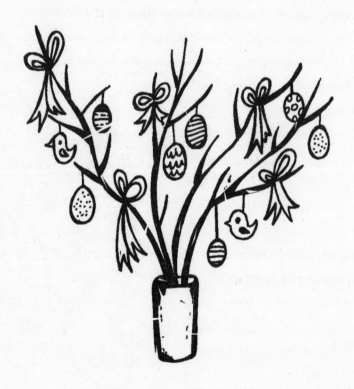

In the Spring

1. Before you start it's worth taking a bit of time to find the perfect branch for your tree. Fallen branches that have smaller branches attached are ideal, as they'll give you something to hang your decorations on. If you can't find a branch, sturdy twigs will work just as well.
2. Instead of using fallen branches, you could also cut branches from a tree and put them in a jug of water in the house. If the branches have buds, your Easter tree will look even more special when they open up.
3. Once you have your tree, put it in your plant pot. Make sure the pot is deep enough to support your tree, and fill it with gravel, sand or pebbles to stop it toppling over.
4. To decorate your tree you could tie ribbons to the branches in bright spring colours like yellow and green.

There are some different ideas for decorations to hang on your tree on the next few pages.

Blown Eggs

This is a wonderful skill to learn – it's quite fiddly but well worth it! You might need an adult to help you at first.

1. Make a small hole in each end of your egg with a drawing pin. You'll have to push quite hard, but don't worry about cracking the shell – the ends of an egg are the strongest parts.
2. Use the pin to carefully make one of the holes a little larger – about ⅛ in (3 mm) across.
3. With a bowl underneath, blow through the smaller hole until insides of the egg come out of the bigger hole. You will have to blow very hard at first! Keep blowing until all the egg has come out and then rinse under the tap. Dry your egg well with kitchen paper and it is ready to decorate!

Decorating your eggs

Felt-tip pens and acrylic paints work very well for decorating blown eggs, but there are some more exciting ways to do it. You'll need an adult to help you, but the results will be spectacular!

Dyed eggs

You can use lots of different things to add colour to your egg – some vegetables have wonderful colours in them. You can make purple with red cabbage, pink with beetroot and orange with carrots. Put your chosen vegetable into boiling water with a teaspoon of vinegar, return to the boil and reduce the heat to simmer.

When the water is a good deep colour, strain it into a heat-proof bowl and leave it to cool.

Lower your eggs gently into the dye and leave them until their shells change colour. Lift them out with a slotted spoon and leave to dry.

You could also use food colouring to dye your eggs in more or less the same way – just add a couple of drops to a bowl of hot water along with a teaspoon of vinegar, then continue as above.

Waxed eggs

To make your eggs look even more
special, draw a design on them using
a crayon or candle before you dye
them. The dye won't stick to the
parts where you've drawn. You can
even add a second colour – ask an
adult to put your dyed eggs in the
oven (heated to 200 degrees C/
gas 6) for a few minutes until the wax has
melted, then soak them in another colour.

To hang your eggs, wrap a length of ribbon around each
one, using glue or double-sided tape to stick it down, then tie
in a bow at the top. If you don't want to hang them from your
tree, you can display them in egg cups!

Felt Eggs

Felt is very useful as you can either sew or simply glue pieces together. These eggs are easy to prepare and make good Easter gifts.

You will need:
Felt
PVA glue
Ribbons
Sequins

1. Cut two egg-shaped pieces out of felt.
2. Make a loop of ribbon and sandwich the ends between the two pieces of felt, sticking it all together with PVA glue.
3. Glue on small bows made from ribbon, or sequins.

Make a Duckling

And it was not very long before Milly-Molly-Mandy had saved up to threepence; and then Uncle let her have a little yellow baby duckling all for her own.
Milly-Molly-Mandy Spends a Penny

Here's an easy way to make your own little paper duckling that actually hatches from its own egg!

You will need:
Two small paper plates
Paint, pens and decoration
Yellow cardboard
Googly eyes
Glue
A paper fastener
Stapler

1. The paper plates will be your egg, so decide what colour you want it to be and how you want to decorate it. Then paint or colour both plates front and back and leave to dry.
2. Now draw a duckling shape on the cardboard and cut it out. Make sure it is slightly smaller than the plates, so it will fit snugly inside.
3. You could use yellow felt or fabric instead for the duckling – if it's too floppy, stick it on cardboard first.

4. Make some eyes for your duckling. Googly eyes work well, but don't worry if you haven't got any – cardboard will do just as well.

5. Next make its beak. The best way to do this is to cut a small circle and fold it in half. Glue one half of the circle on to the chick, right under the eyes. Then the beak should jut out, just like a real duck's beak.

6. Now go back to your plates. Cut one in half in a jagged line to look like an egg that has just broken open. Then hinge the two pieces back together on one side, using the paper fastener.

7. Next staple the bottom half of the hinged plate on to the other paper plate.

8. Now you should have a paper-plate pocket with a hinged front that opens like an egg cracking open.

9. Put your duckling inside, and it's finished. When you open the egg, your duckling will look as if it is hatching.

Glove Puppet Bunny Rabbit

And suddenly – what do you think they saw? A little ball of brown fur, just ahead of them among the grasses in the ditch.

"Is it a rabbit?" whispered Little-friend-Susan.

Milly-Molly-Mandy Goes Blackberrying

If you lose a glove, don't throw the other one away – make another puppet to add to your collection!

You will need:
A glove
Needle and thread
Buttons
Felt
A cotton wool ball or white pompom
More cotton wool for stuffing (optional)

1. Turn your glove inside out and sew together the thumb and the middle two fingers. Turn the glove the right way out again and push out the two fingers that you didn't sew up – these are your bunny's ears!

2. Now give your bunny a face. You can stick on pieces of felt, or use wool to sew eyes and a nose.

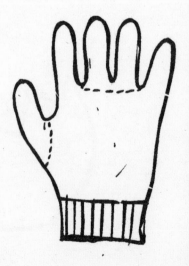

3. To make your bunny's tail you could either make a small white pompom (see pages 222–25) or glue a cotton wool ball to the back of your puppet.
4. You could also stuff your puppet with cotton wool and sew up the bottom to make a cuddly toy that you can keep.

Spring Daffodils

Daffodils are such friendly flowers – they pop up everywhere when spring arrives. You can make your own daffodils very easily and they will last a lot longer than the real thing!

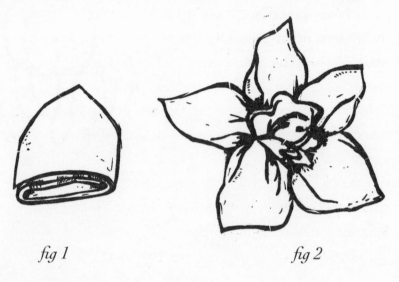

fig 1   *fig 2*

You will need:
Yellow and green crêpe paper
An A4 sheet of green paper or thin card for each daffodil
Sticky tape
Scissors

1. Roll your sheet of green paper into a tight tube by laying it flat on the table and rolling from the top left corner to the bottom right. Secure the end with tape. This is your stalk.
2. Crêpe paper normally comes rolled up. Cut the end off your yellow roll so that you have a long strip about 3 in (8 cm) wide, and unroll it.

3. Fold the paper up again loosely so that you have about five layers, then cut an oval shape into the top. This will be your outer petals (*as fig 1*).

4. Do the same thing again, but this time your strip should be about 1½ in (4 cm) wide. Fold it so that you have about ten layers, and cut a wavy line along the top. This will be your inner petals.

5. Take your inner petals and tape one end to the top of your stalk. Wind the strip around the stalk, fluffing out the petals as you go. Secure the other end with tape.

6. Now do the same with the outer petals. When you have finished, arrange and pinch the petals so that they look more realistic (*as fig 2*).

7. To make leaves, roll up some green crêpe paper and cut into a tall point. Wrap around the stem of your daffodil and secure with tape.

Muvver's Day Plant Pot

Milly-Molly-Mandy loves making things for people – particularly her mother. This plant pot would make a perfect Mother's Day gift or a present for a spring birthday. You can make it as simple or as complicated as you like. Here's how to do it.

You will need:

A terracotta pot

Acrylic paint

PVA glue

Decoration: shells, buttons, small pebbles, beads or dried flowers.

1. First, make sure your pot is clean. Rinse off any soil or dust. Then, when it is completely dry, paint it all over with acrylic paint. You can use any colour you like, though a lighter colour would be easier if you wanted to add any other painted decoration to it later.

2. When your base colour is dry, paint a pattern on top. Hearts, stars, spots or flowers work well. Be careful not

to smudge your design when you turn it round to do the other sides.

3. As well as painting a design, you could make a pattern using beads, shells, small pebbles or even dried flowers. Start by spreading a thick layer of PVA glue on to your pot, then carefully stick on your decoration. When your design is finished, add a final layer of glue to make sure your decoration is fixed on firmly and leave it to dry.

4. When your pot is finished, you could put a plant inside to make it even more special.

Paper Basket

This basket is very easy to make once you know how, and could be used for all sorts of things. You could fill it with sweets as a gift, or use it to carry your Easter eggs!

You will need:
Paper
Stapler

You might want to choose some nice coloured paper. If you don't have any, why not colour the paper yourself?

1. Fold your piece of paper in half, short ends together. Repeat, laying the folded edge over the open ends, so that when you open it up there are four long rectangles. Then fold each long edge into the centre of the paper. When you open it, you should find that there are 16 squares (*as fig 1*).

2. Bring the top and bottom flaps into the centre of the piece of paper and then fold each corner down two-thirds of the way to the centre line (*as fig 2*).

3. Next fold the remaining third over so that the corners are tucked in on both sides. Hold the centre of the two sides and gently pull them apart (*as fig 3*).

4. Now pinch each corner from top to bottom and you will see the shape of your box forming!

5. You should now cut a wide strip of paper for a handle and staple the ends to either side of your new basket.

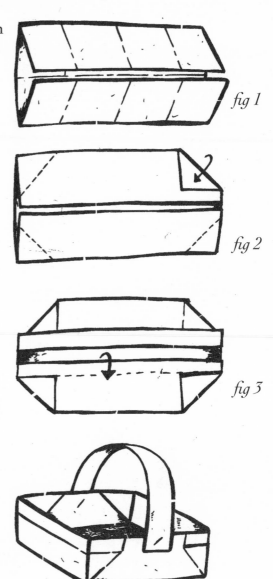

fig 1

fig 2

fig 3

Things to Make and Do in the Summer

And it was the most beautiful, quiet summer
morning that ever was.

   "Well!" said Milly-Molly-Mandy to herself.
"It's much too beautiful a morning to stay in bed
till breakfast time."
Milly-Molly-Mandy Gets Up Early

Whether it's picnics on the beach, camping in the garden or
just picking a few flowers to dry into posies, Milly-Molly-
Mandy always makes the most of the long summer days. You
can join in the fun too with these exciting activities.

Camping Out

Billy Blunt had spread an old mackintosh for a ground-sheet, and there was a box in one corner to hold a bottle of water and a mug, and his electric torch . . . and when the front flap of the tent was closed you couldn't see anything outside, except a tiny bit of sky . . .
Milly-Molly-Mandy Camps Out

When Milly-Molly-Mandy sees Billy's tent, she can't resist having a go herself. She and Little-friend-Susan make their own tent in the garden, and eventually all three camp out for the night.

In the Summer

Sleeping under the stars is a marvellous experience in the summertime, and you don't need to go far to try it. If you have a tent and a secure back garden, you have the ideal place to camp out for a night – though you'll need a grown-up or a much older brother or sister to do it with you.

Once you've pitched your tent, make it comfortable with sleeping bags, cushions and blankets. Don't forget a torch and some snacks. (You could even have a barbecue before bedtime.) Also, take some warm clothes – even if it's been a hot day, the temperature will drop at night.

Then snuggle up and watch the stars. Tell stories and sing songs.

> **And the trees outside grew slowly blacker and blacker until they couldn't be seen at all; and the owls hooted; and a faraway cow moo-ed . . . and then at last they all fell fast asleep.**
> *Milly-Molly-Mandy Camps Out*

When you wake up in the morning, you'll be amazed by the noises you'll hear – noises that you don't normally notice like the sound of the trees rustling, the birds singing and the buzzing of insects. The grass smells different too – fresh and slightly damp.

> **. . . and then Little-friend-Susan and Billy Blunt, in their pyjamas, crawled out and ran about too (because it feels so very nice, and sort of new, to be running about under the sky in your pyjamas!).**
> *Milly-Molly-Mandy Camps Out*

Pick-a-posy

When Great-Aunty Margaret saw the flowers on
her chest of drawers she said gently:
"Why, Millicent Margaret Amanda, I believe that
is your doing! Thank you, my dearie!"
Milly-Molly-Mandy Meets her Great-Aunt

Enjoy summer flowers all year round by making a dried posy.

You will need:
Fresh flowers
Elastic band
A clothes peg

1. First you need to pick your flowers. (Remember to ask
   first.) Choose ones that are in the
   early stages of blooming;
   those which are just
   opening out are best. If
   you try to dry flowers
   that are well past their
   best, the petals may fall
   off.
2. When you have gathered
   your posy, pull off some of the
   lower leaves (not the ones close to
   the flower head) and dry off any
   dampness.

194

3. Then tie your posy together with the elastic band. Don't use string – when the flowers dry they shrink and could fall out of the string, whereas the elastic band will shrink with them.

4. Now find somewhere dark and dry like a store room or a garage. Hang your posy there, upside down, using your clothes peg. You will need to leave it for about two to three weeks.

5. Once the posy is completely dried, try hanging it in a window, or put it in a pretty vase on a window ledge. Posies also make lovely gifts.

❀ ❀ ❀ **TIP** ❀ ❀ ❀

Why not try growing your own flowers to make posies? Sow seeds in the spring and they'll be ready to cut in the summer.

❀ ❀ ❀

Make a Buttercup or Daisy Chain

There was nobody to see them now but the cows, so they ran, laughing and giggling and tumbling against each other among the buttercups all the way across.

Milly-Molly-Mandy Dresses Up

There's nothing nicer than sitting on the grass on a sunny day and making a chain of flowers. Have a competition to see who can make the longest chain, or make one just long enough to wear as a fairy crown.

You will need:
Lots of daisies or buttercups
Your thumbnail (which should be quite long – a good reason to stop biting your nails!)
A sunny day

1. Pick flowers with good long stalks, and make a slit about halfway down the stalk of your first flower with your thumbnail – all the way through to the other side.
2. Thread your next flower through the hole in your first, and pull it through until the flower head is up against the stalk.
3. Now make a slit in the stalk of your second flower, and thread your third flower through it. Continue until you have a nice long chain.

❀ ❀ ❀ **TIP** ❀ ❀ ❀

If you want to join one end of your chain to the other, make a slightly longer slit in the stem of your last flower, and gently push the head of your first flower through it. You will need to be very careful not to split the stem too far!

❀ ❀ ❀

Pressed Flowers

Little-friend-Susan had a bunch of flowers from her garden, marigolds and Michaelmas daisies, and nasturtiums.
Milly-Molly-Mandy and the Surprise Plant

Pressed flowers can be just as pretty as fresh ones, and look lovely stuck to paper as greetings cards.

You will need:
Flowers
A flower press or heavy book with blotting paper between
    the pages

1. First you need to find some flowers. Those with separate petals work best. Make sure they are in good condition and dry them off before you press them. (It's sometimes easier to remove the stems and leaves and dry them all separately, then put them back together afterwards.)

2. Use a flower press, or make your own by pressing the flowers in between the pages of a heavy book. Make sure you put a sheet of blotting paper above and below them so that they don't mark your book.

3. It will usually take about two weeks for them to be fully pressed. Tighten your press every few days as the flowers shrink when they dry out. If you're using a book, you could place another book on top of the first after a few days.

 TIP
You don't need expensive flowers to press.
Small flowering weeds work just as well.

Lavender Bags

And Aunty brought out of her small top drawer some most beautiful pink ribbon, all smelling of Lavender – just enough to make into a sash for the party frock.
Milly-Molly-Mandy Goes to a Party

Lavender is easy to grow and smells wonderful. If you've got some in your garden, this is a good way to make use of it – pick a few stalks and turn them into beautiful lavender bags. They are perfect to tuck inside a drawer to keep your clothes smelling nice, or try putting one inside a cushion or a pillow. They make lovely gifts.

You will need:
Dried lavender
Circles of fabric about 6–8 inches (15–20 cm) wide
Ribbon

1. Fresh lavender is easy to dry. Use the same method as the dried flower posy: pick a few stems just before they bloom and hang them to dry for a week or two in a cool, dark, dry place.
2. When they are fully dried out, put a newspaper on the ground, then run your hand over the stems to knock off the little buds of lavender. You will need about a tablespoonful to make a lavender bag.

3. Next, take your circle of fabric and put a spoonful of lavender in the middle.

4. Now gather it up and tie the ribbon tightly around the neck. Make a pretty bow. If you have any fabric flowers or decorations you could glue or sew them on to the ribbon.

❖ If you haven't got lavender growing in your garden, you can buy it already dried from shops.

Lavender Water

Aunty had a new mauve silk scarf for her neck, and a newly trimmed hat, and her handkerchief was sprinkled with the lavender-water that Milly-Molly-Mandy had given her last Christmas.

Milly-Molly-Mandy felt so proud that it was being used for such a special occasion.

Milly-Molly-Mandy Goes to a Concert

You will need:

A wide-necked screw-top jar, such as a jam jar

Three handfuls of dried lavender flowers

1 cup of white wine vinegar

Half a cup of rose water

1. Put all the ingredients into the jar and screw the lid on tightly.
2. Keep the jar in a dark place, and shake it frequently.
3. After 2–3 weeks you can strain the mixture into pretty little bottles and make nice labels for them.

Make a Boat

And there was the sea, all jumping with sparkles in the sunshine, as far as ever you could see.
Milly-Molly-Mandy Goes to the Sea

There's something very peaceful about sailing little boats on a summer's day. You don't need a pond or a river to do it – a paddling pool or plastic basin with a few inches of water is just as good. If the weather's bad you could use the kitchen sink, or even save them for bath-time. Here are two simple ways to make a boat.

Paper or foil boats

1. You will need a rectangle of paper or kitchen foil. Experiment until you get the size you want, but A4 works well.
2. Lay the piece of paper in front of you with the short side at the top. Fold the top edge down to meet the bottom edge and crease. Fold the left side to meet the right side, crease, and then unfold at that crease. Fold the top left and right corners down to meet at the middle and crease. There are two strips of paper below the two triangles you have just made. Fold the top strip up and crease, then turn the paper over and repeat. At this point it will look a lot like a paper hat! (*as fig 1*)

3. Rotate the paper so the point of the triangle is on one side. Pick it up and open the triangle, keeping your thumbs inside.

4. As you open it up, it will flatten into a diamond shape. Tuck in stray flaps, if any, and crease (*as fig 2*).

5. Fold one bottom point up to meet the top point of the diamond, crease, then turn the paper over and repeat. Again rotate the triangle and open it, flattening it into a diamond shape.

6. As shown in the diagram, pick up the diamond and gently pull the sides apart (*as fig 3*).

7. When they won't pull apart any more, flatten into a canoe shape (*as fig 4*).

8. If you want to make your boat extra waterproof, cover the bottom with sticky tape.

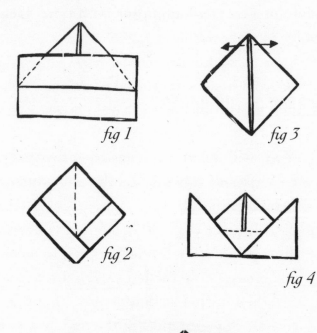

fig 1

fig 3

fig 2

fig 4

Margarine tub boats

These boats are a bit more robust – and they can take passengers. Little plastic people would fit inside easily.

All you need is an empty margarine tub, a small blob of plasticine or Blu-tack, a straw, and tissue paper to make a sail.

Start by making your sail. Cut out a triangle or rectangle shape from tissue paper. Make two small holes down one side of your shape, and thread your straw through them to make the sail.

Press your blob of plasticine or Blu-tack in the centre of your margarine tub and stick your straw firmly into it. Now you're ready to sail!

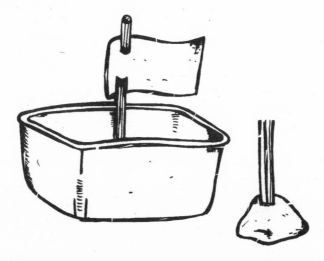

Go to the Beach

Mother told Milly-Molly-Mandy about the splashy waves and the sand and the little crabs, and Milly-Molly-Mandy just longed to go there herself.
Milly-Molly-Mandy Goes to the Sea

Nothing quite beats a day on the beach with sand, sun and perhaps an ice cream or two. You don't have to have a sunny day to enjoy the beach. It can be just as much fun on a grey day, when you will probably have the sand to yourself. Here are some ideas to try, whatever the weather.

Fly a kite

The beach is a perfect place to learn to fly a kite. You can buy one fairly cheaply, or have a go at making one. Here's an idea to try.

You will need:
Sticks or garden canes
Crêpe or tissue paper
Masking tape

String
Ribbon if you have it
Cardboard for the handle

1. Find two sticks or thin canes (one shorter than the other). Lay the smaller one across the longer one, about a third of the way down, to make a cross. Now bind them together tightly with string or masking tape.
2. Ask an adult to cut a small notch into the ends of each stick, about ¼ in (0.5 cm) deep for the string to fit into.
3. Make a loop in one end of the string, then tie that end around the end of the cane at the top of your kite, leaving the loop free. Now wind the string around the other three cane ends, through the notches you've made, so that it makes your cross into a diamond shape. Make a small loop in the string at the bottom of the kite to match the one at the top. The string should be taut, but not so tight that it makes the canes bend (*as fig 1*).

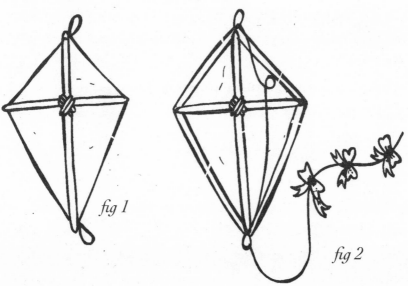

fig 1

fig 2

4. Lay your kite on the tissue paper, then cut around it, so that you have a diamond shape that is a bit bigger than your kite.

5. Fold the excess paper over the string and glue or tape it to itself.

6. When it is dry, cut a piece of string about 4 ft (122 cm) long and tie one end to the loop at the top of the kite. Tie another small loop in the string just above the intersection of the two cross-pieces. This will be the kite's bridle, the string to which the flying line is attached. Now thread the other end of the string through the loop at the bottom of the kite and secure it.

7. Make a tail by tying a small ribbon roughly every 4 in (10 cm) along the length of string. Attach the tail to the loop at the bottom of the kite.

8. Finally, attach a long piece of string to the loop in the middle of your kite. Wind the other end on to a piece of strong cardboard, making sure the end is stuck on to the card with masking tape (*as fig 2*).

9. Now you're ready to brave the beach, though watch out for very strong winds. You may find your home-made kite isn't strong enough to fly on really windy days.

Build a sand castle sculpture

Building sandcastles is a great way to spend an afternoon. Start off by collecting some pieces of driftwood and shells to decorate your castle, then get building. Try making a moat round your castle, then add a village outside the moat . . .

or even a large town of sand buildings.

You could also try making sand sculptures. These can be anything you like. Objects with a sea theme are fun: starfish, sea turtles, mermaids or even a boat that is big enough to sit in.

Sand games

The beach is a bit like having a large blank sheet of paper. All you need is a stick and then you can draw or write all over the wet sand!

Try playing giant noughts and crosses or hangman. Make your own sand maze or play a simple word game, where you draw an object and your friends have to guess what it is.

You could also make a sand trail for your friends to follow, with arrows and messages written in the sand, and "treasure" – perhaps a pretty shell – buried at the end.

Scavenger hunt

You never know what you might find washed up on the beach. A fun activity is to hold a scavenger hunt, where you think up a list of objects such as different sized shells, interesting stones, unusual driftwood, seaweed or starfish, and everyone tries to find them. The first one to finish is the winner. You could also have a special prize for the most unusual find.

✿ ✿ ✿ TIP ✿ ✿ ✿
Take a plain white tray to the beach with you,
and when you have collected a bucket full of
interesting beach creatures, pour them carefully
on to the tray so that you can see them better.

Rock-pooling

And then they played and explored among the rock-pools and had tea on the sand.
Milly-Molly-Mandy Goes to the Sea

Take a bucket and spend a few hours hunting through rock pools, looking at all the interesting creatures that live in them. Carefully move stones to see what's underneath. Look out for small crabs and fish, tiny shrimps, limpets and starfish. Be sure to put them back carefully when you've finished looking.

Hold a Sale

. . . so Milly-Molly-Mandy fetched a pencil and paper and wrote out very carefully: Millicent Margaret Amanda and Susan & co. have bunches of flowers for sale and clean brass very cheap (we do not spill the polish) and run errands very cheap.

Milly-Molly-Mandy Gives a Party

Sometimes you might want to earn some extra pocket money – or raise money for a good cause. This is the perfect way to do just that, and have a jolly good clean-out, all at the same time!

First, decide what to sell. You could follow Milly-Molly-Mandy's example and sell things from your garden, such as flowers, fruit, plants or vegetables (though do ask first), or you could hold a jumble sale and sell off unwanted toys, books or games.

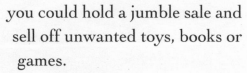

Old clothes can be sold, or bagged up and taken to your local charity shop (though be sure to save any attractive pieces of material for your ragbag or craft box).

Special toys that you've grown out of can be passed on to younger friends or brothers and sisters. Anything else you don't need can be boxed up ready to sell. Be sure to check that all jigsaws are complete and nothing is too dog-eared!

Decide when to hold your sale. Saturdays are good, when lots of people will be around. You could make leaflets to tell people about it – it's best to keep them simple and bright. It's a good idea to hold your sale in your front garden or driveway, where passers-by will see it too.

Consider selling a variety of things. As well as unwanted toys and games, sell things you've made or grown: colourful bookmarks, dried flowers, lavender bags, seedlings from your garden or fruit and vegetables. (Have a look in the craft and gardening sections of this book for more ideas.)

A lovely idea would be to have a charity sale, and donate all the money you raise to a good cause.

Make a Summer Scrapbook

This is a good way to remember what you did in the summer. Picnics, day trips, visiting friends, or just butterfly spotting on a sunny afternoon in the garden – whatever you get up to, keep a record of it in your summer scrapbook.

To get started, all you need is an empty notebook or several sheets of paper fastened together. Just make a hole in the top and bottom corner of all your sheets of paper and tie them together with string or a ribbon.

You'll also need glue to stick anything interesting inside, and pens to decorate the cover and draw pictures.

On the inside of the first page you might like to write a bit about yourself; such as what you like to eat, your favourite TV programmes or who your best friends are. Perhaps you could include the names of your family and pets too. Then draw a picture of yourself underneath.

Each day try to add something new to your scrapbook. You could start by writing the day and the date on each page, then draw a weather

picture to show if it was sunny or wet that day. Then describe what you did.

If you go anywhere, try to bring back something small to stick inside your scrapbook. For example, if you go to a museum, pick up a leaflet about it or buy a small postcard. If you visit the park or the woods, bring back a nice leaf, or a twig or some bark from a tree. At the beach, look out for small shells or seaweed. Always keep cinema or bus tickets and if you visit a cafe bring home the receipt.

If you've got a camera you could take pictures to put in your book too.

On days when you're at home, draw what you see in the garden: colourful butterflies, dragonflies and other insects, birds, squirrels and rabbits.

If you like to cook, write your favourite recipes inside, or draw a picture of whatever you've made.

By the end of the summer you'll have a lovely journal to keep and show, and you'll always remember the fun things you did.

Things to Make and Do
in the Autumn

Father was very busy, digging up potatoes and cutting down dead plants and burning rubbish on a big bonfire. So Milly-Molly-Mandy was very busy too, sweeping up leaves and picking up tools which Father dropped and throwing bits on to the bonfire.

(Autumn is a very busy time in the garden.)

Milly-Molly-Mandy Cooks a Dinner

The days are getting shorter, the weather is turning chilly and the leaves are starting to fall off the trees. Autumn's arrived, and there are lots of exciting craft ideas to make use of all those beautiful leaves and pine cones.

Leaf-print Pictures

. . . so they amused themselves by walking in a dry ditch close by the fence, shuffling along in the leaves with their stout little boots that were to have kept the prickles off.
Milly-Molly-Mandy Goes Blackberrying

Autumn leaves look so lovely on the trees – this easy printing project is a nice way to capture their beauty.

You will need:
A selection of different leaves
Paint – reds, yellows and greens work well
Paper
Black marker pen

1. Choose different shapes and sizes of leaf. Look on the back – the leaves with the most prominent vein patterns will make the best prints.

2. Carefully brush paint on the underside of your leaf. Not too much, or you won't be able to see the pattern when you print.

3. Press the leaf down firmly on your paper, and rub gently over the top. Peel off the leaf and you should have a lovely leaf print. Don't worry if you can't get all the detail of the leaf at first because it can take time to get a really good print. You may need to experiment a little with the right amount of paint and how hard to press.

4. You can always wait until your prints are dry, and then highlight the leaf details with a black marker pen.

5. Once you've got the hang of it, repeat with your other leaves.

6. Try making patterns – or turn your leaf shapes into animals. Choose a leaf with a strong shape, and turn it into a hedgehog, mouse, bird or butterfly. Once the print has dried, use a black marker pen to add details like eyes, spikes, whiskers, etc.

7. You could also use the leaves as stencils by laying them on a sheet of paper then painting over the whole sheet. When you lift the leaves, there will be a white leaf shape left behind!
Stencilling also works well with sponge painting. Instead of using a brush to paint over the leaves, use a small piece of old sponge dipped in paint.

Family Tree

"Is she my great-aunty and your sister too?" she asked Grandma.

"Yes, and she's my sister-in-law," said Grandpa.

"And my aunty," said Mother.

"And my aunty-in-law," said Father.

"And my aunty-in-law too," said Aunty.

"And my aunty," said Uncle.

"Fancy!" said Milly-Molly-Mandy. "She's all that, and she's a great-aunty too!"

Milly-Molly-Mandy Meets her Great-Aunt

This is a great way to find out where you come from. Make your own family tree, using real leaves to write all your family's names on.

You will need:

A large sheet of paper

Small autumn leaves

Sticky labels (or small pieces of paper with rolled-up sticky tape on the back)

Felt-tip pens

1. The first thing you need to do is draw a large tree shape, or cut one out of brown tissue paper. Your tree should be wider at the bottom than it is at the top. Give it lots of lovely branches and colour it in.

2. Now decide how far back in your family tree you want to go. You could start with your grandparents or perhaps even your great-grandparents.

3. Whoever you want to start with, write each of their names on a different leaf shape, and then stick them right at the top of your tree.

4. If you started with your grandparents, write your parents' names on leaves and stick them on the next branch down, with any of your aunts and uncles. Then put yourself on the branch below, along with any of your brothers or sisters or cousins.

Pompom Hedgehog

So Milly-Molly-Mandy carried the baby hedgehog between her two hands very carefully; and it unrolled itself a bit and quivered its little soft nose over her fingers as if it hoped they might be good to eat, and it squeaked and squeaked, because it was very hungry.
Milly-Molly-Mandy Minds a Baby

Why not make yourself a pet hedgehog just like Milly-Molly-Mandy's . . . out of pompoms! The winding part of the pompom can take a bit of time, but the end result is more than worth the effort.

You will need:
Cardboard
A mug and an egg cup to draw round
Brown wool
Cream or white felt for the face
Black pen and cardboard to make eyes and a nose
A small cardboard box and
    twigs or leaves to make a
    home for your pet

1. Use the mug to draw two circles on the cardboard.
2. Use the egg cup to draw two smaller circles inside the larger circles
3. Ask a grown-up to cut out the two larger circles, and then cut out their middles – you should now have two holey shapes that look like doughnuts.
4. Put the two circles together and tie your wool on to them, then start winding the wool around them, pushing it through the middle of the circles. This will be much easier if you have a wool needle with a large eye. To make the process quicker,

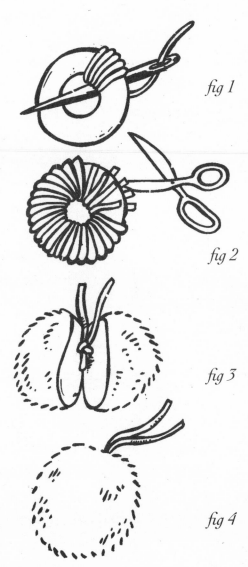

fig 1

fig 2

fig 3

fig 4

you could cut lots of long pieces of wool and wind them four or five at a time (*as fig 1*).

5. Keep winding until the central hole completely disappears.

6. Use nail scissors to snip through the wool around the outside edge of the circles. This is fiddly, so ask a grown-up to help (*as fig 2*).

7. When you've snipped all the way around, pull the cardboard circles apart a little way and tie a length of wool round the middle of the ball, between the two circles, to secure your pompom. Tie and knot tightly (*as fig 3*).

8. Cut or pull off the cardboard and fluff up your pompom. You may need to neaten it up a little by snipping the ends with some nail scissors (*as fig 4*).

9. Now make a cone shape out of white felt for your hedgehog's face.

10. Decorate it with eyes and a black nose and then glue on to your pompom. If your glue isn't strong enough, ask a grown-up to sew the face on for you.

11. Add felt feet to the bottom.

 TIP

Larger balls of wool sometimes get in a tangle, so cut long pieces of wool and wind them into mini balls. When one runs out, just tie on another and keep winding! To make larger pompoms, use bigger cardboard circles.

❀ ❀ ❀

To make a pompom snowman, glue together two white pompoms of slightly different sizes and glue together. Cut out cardboard eyes, a carrot nose and buttons. Knit or use a ribbon for a scarf, twist and wind a pipe cleaner for arms and make a hat out of cardboard and the cap from a plastic bottle.

Make chicks from yellow pompoms. Cut out cardboard beaks and eyes and glue them on. Fill a box with brown and green tissue paper leaves and sticks (or use real ones from the garden) to make into a nest for your chicks.

Scary Pumpkin Candle

This is a lovely alternative to carving a pumpkin at Halloween, and can be put in your window to show that you're expecting trick-or-treaters!

You will need:
A glass jar
Orange tissue paper
PVA glue
A black marker pen or black paper
A tea light

1. Cover your glass jar with a layer of PVA glue, thinned down with a little water.
2. Tear the tissue paper into small pieces, stick them all over your jar so that there are no gaps, and leave to dry.
3. Add a scary pumpkin face with a black marker pen or by gluing on pieces of black paper.
4. Place the tea light inside the jar and ask an adult to light it – your pumpkin will glow beautifully!
5. You could choose different coloured tissue paper or sweet wrappers to make other designs – use your imagination!

Billy Blunt's Pine-cone Forecaster

Billy Blunt is a real outdoors boy, and knows a thing or two about nature. In the autumn he collects pine cones. They're great for craft – but they're also useful for predicting the weather. Hang one up outside your house, where you can see it from the window. When there's wet weather on the way, your pine cone should close up tightly, and it will reopen in dry weather.

Harvest Mouse Finger Puppet

Here's a quick way to make a friendly little finger puppet.

You will need:
Pencil
A cup to draw round
Cardboard or paper
Scissors
Sticky tape
Felt-tip pen
A pipe cleaner, ribbon or string for the tail

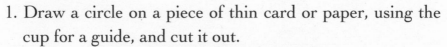

1. Draw a circle on a piece of thin card or paper, using the cup for a guide, and cut it out.
2. Make a cut from the edge of the circle to the centre, then roll it into a cone shape, and fasten with sticky tape.
3. Cut out two ear shapes and sticky-tape them on.
4. Draw black eyes, a nose and some whiskers on your mouse's face.
5. Sticky-tape a tail on to the inside of the cone, using a pipe cleaner, a ribbon or some string.
6. And that's it! Your mouse is finished.

❖ If you have any old yellow sponges lying around, you could cut off a corner to make some cheese for your mouse – or make some out of yellow cardboard. Ask a grown-up to hole-punch a few holes into it, to make it look really cheesy.

 **TIP**
**Why not make a family of mice,
and sticky-tape them on to the fingers of an old
glove. Then you could put on a puppet show!**

Fireworks Etching

There was a great bang! and a whoosh! And showers of beautiful stars lit up everything. And what with the roaring of the bonfire and the banging of the fireworks and the shouts of Milly-Molly-Mandy and Little-friend-Susan and Billy Blunt, anyone would know they had a splendid Guy Fawkes celebration.

Milly-Molly-Mandy and Guy Fawkes Day

This is a very satisfying and rather messy way to make a splendid fireworks picture. Make sure you have a spare black crayon handy!

You will need:
Newspaper
A sheet of white paper
Some coloured felt-tip pens
Black crayons
Something to scratch with – a
   toothpick, cocktail stick or chopstick
   will all work well

1. Spread out some newspaper to protect the surface you're working on, then cover your sheet of paper with lots of colourful patterns. It doesn't really

matter what you draw, but the more colourful, the better!

2. Now for the messy part – cover the whole sheet of paper in a thick layer of black crayon, so that you can't see any of the colour at all. Try to go right to the edges (this is when the newspaper is handy) and make the black even all over.

3. When you've covered the paper or run out of black crayons (whichever comes first), you can draw your fireworks. If you scratch through the layer of black, the beautiful colours beneath will shine through – you could draw stars, Catherine wheels, rockets and even sparklers!

Pine-cone Bird Feeder

Pine cones also make great bird feeders. Here's how to do it.

You will need:
A pine cone
Ribbon or string
Vegetable suet or lard
Bird seed

1. Tie the ribbon or string around the pine cone, then mix lots of bird seed into the suet or lard.
2. Spread the seed mixture all over the pine cone, stuffing it firmly into the gaps.
3. Hang outside for the birds to enjoy.

Things to Make and Do in the Winter

It was such a cold wintry day that everybody turned up their coat-collars and put their hands in their pockets, and such a grey wintry day that it seemed almost dark already, though it was only four o'clock.
Milly-Molly-Mandy Goes Sledging

Milly-Molly Mandy loves the snow. But when the weather turns chilly, she's more than happy to cosy up indoors with her craft box. Here are some ideas for lovely wintry things to do when it's cold outside!

Orange Pomander

This pretty decoration smells lovely and looks great hanging on a Christmas tree.

You will need:
An orange
Whole cloves
Ribbon

1. Cut two lengths of ribbon and wrap them round the orange. Tie at the top, then make a loop with the ends.
2. Your orange should now have four quarters to decorate with cloves.
3. If your orange is soft, you should be able to stick the cloves straight into it. If not, ask a grown-up to puncture some holes in the skin with a sharp cocktail stick, a skewer or the end of a knitting needle.
4. Stick the cloves firmly into the skin of the orange. You can make any pattern you like, but lines running down the sides work well and look nice and neat.

5. When you've finished, hang your pomander on the tree or put it in a drawer – it will make everything smell lovely and will last for years!

Soon Mother beckoned to Milly-Molly-Mandy from behind Father's shoulder, and Mr Moggs to Little-friend-Susan. They knew that meant bed, but for once they didn't much mind, because it would make Christmas come all the sooner!

Milly-Molly-Mandy Goes Carol-Singing

Make a Cosy Snowman Card

She and Little-friend-Susan had a grand time all that afternoon, making a snowman in the Moggs' front garden.

Milly-Molly-Mandy Goes Sledging

This snowman card is perfect for Christmas – with a real knitted hat and scarf to keep him warm. Here's how to do it.

You will need:
White cardboard
Coloured paper (gold if you have it)
Decoration: silver glitter
Wool and knitting needles
A tiny pompom
Glue

1. Make a card shape out of white cardboard. Cut out a square of coloured paper slightly smaller than the card and stick it in the centre of the front. If you have fancy scissors with patterned blades, you could use them to give your paper a zigzag edge.
2. Draw a snowman on white cardboard. Cut it out and stick it in the centre of the coloured paper.
3. Now for the knitting. (If you find this too fiddly, ask a grown-up to help.)
4. To make the scarf, cast on 6 stitches and start knitting. Keep knitting until your scarf is long enough for your

snowman – about 2–3 in (5–8 cm). Cast off and glue the scarf on to the neck of your snowman, so that it hangs down his front. Use a felt-tip pen in the same colour as the scarf to draw in the tassels.

5. Next, make the hat by casting on 6 stitches. Knit 6 rows, then decrease by knitting two stitches together at the start and end of the next 2 rows. Knit the last two stitches together, and cast off. Glue the hat on to the top of your snowman's head. Add the pompom to the top of the hat.

6. Decorate your snowman's face with felt-tip pens and draw on some arms. Add some blobs of glue around your snowman, and shake on some glitter for sparkly snow falling. Add some more around his feet.

Pop-up Christmas Tree Card

Here's another special Christmas card. This one has a secret surprise inside – a pop-up Christmas tree!

You will need:
Thick card
Green foam or green card
Glitter
Glue
Double-sided sticky tape
Pens

1. Cut two rectangles of cardboard. Fold them in half into a card shape. Put one aside for later. It will be the backing card.
2. Make two short cuts in the front of the first card, starting at the fold, to make a flap. Fold the flap down and crease well. Then fold it the other way and crease again.
3. Put the flap back in its place, then open the card and press the flap down into the inside of the card.
4. Now, with the flap still down, carefully close the card. When you open it again, the flap should stick out and look like a little step inside your card.

5. Use double-sided sticky tape or glue to fix this card inside the backing card.
6. Now cut out a Christmas tree shape from green cardboard or foam. Make sure it's small enough so that it fits snugly inside the card when it is closed.
7. Before you stick the Christmas tree on, decorate it and the inside and outside of your card using pens, glitter, sequins etc. Then glue or stick the Christmas tree on to the step of your card. And that's it – a lovely card with a secret Christmas surprise!

You can use this design to make lots of different cards – instead of Christmas trees try snowmen, robins, Christmas puddings or crackers.

Finger-paint Snowmen Wrapping Paper

When Father and Grandpa and Uncle had to go out (to see after the cows and the pony and the chickens) they came back looking like snowmen.
Milly-Molly-Mandy Goes Sledging

❀ ❀ ❀ **TIP** ❀ ❀ ❀
If you want larger shapes, try vegetable printing instead. Use chopped-up potatoes or carrots to give you the round shapes you'll need.
❀ ❀ ❀

Home-made wrapping paper is really special and great fun to make. You can also make matching gift tags and Christmas cards.

You will need:
Large sheets of coloured paper or brown wrapping paper
White paint
Felt-tip pens
Silver glitter

1. Lay your large sheet of paper on the table in front of you.
2. To make the snowmen shapes, finger-paint two small

circles, one on top of the other. Repeat this shape all over the paper. When it is almost dry, sprinkle a little glitter over the top of the snowmen, then leave to finish drying.

3. Once the paper is completely dry, use a black felt-tip pen to draw a small top hat on each snowman, some twig-shaped arms, eyes, a mouth and some black buttons. Use an orange pen to make a carrot shape for a nose.

4. To make matching gift tags use a hole-punch to make a hole in one corner of a piece of card and thread through some ribbon or string, so you can attach it to your present. Then decorate in the same way.

❀ ❀ ❀ **TIP** ❀ ❀ ❀
Try finger-painting other designs too: robins, Christmas puddings or Santas. White paper backgrounds would work well with these designs.
❀ ❀ ❀

Pretty Paper Lanterns

These lovely lanterns will brighten up your room – and they take just minutes to make.

You will need:
Sheets of coloured paper
Sticky tape
Scissors
Sticker or glitter to decorate

1. Fold a sheet of paper in half lengthways. Cut a narrow strip off one end to use as a handle later.
2. Make cuts along the folded edge, stopping about 1 in (2.5 cm) from the top.
3. Unfold the piece of paper and turn it inside out, refolding the fold lines.
4. Now tape the two short ends together to make your lantern shape and tape the handle on at the top.

Sparkly Paper Chains

And everywhere looked so pretty, with garlands of coloured paper looped from the ceiling, and everybody in their best clothes.
Milly-Molly-Mandy Goes to a Party

Here is another great way to make your house look more festive. These chains are quick and easy to make and look lovely wrapped around Christmas presents, hung across rooms, or draped round pictures or on the tree.

You will need:
Coloured paper
Sticky tape
Glitter

1. Cut the paper into narrow strips – about 2 in (5 cm) wide.
2. Tape the ends of the first together.
3. Next, loop another strip of paper through the first, and tape its ends together.
4. Carry on with this process until you've made the chain as long as you want.

You can make paper chains out of lots of different types of paper – such as old magazines, last year's Christmas cards – even newspapers, which you can paint before cutting into strips.

Snowflake Decoration

The next day, Sunday, the snow had stopped falling, and it looked beautiful, spread out all over everything.
Milly-Molly-Mandy Goes Sledging

This is an unusual alternative to sticking a bow on a Christmas present. Experiment with different snowflake patterns until you get the shape and style you want. You could also turn them into great gift tags by sticking them on to pieces of sturdy card.

You will need:
Pencil
Coloured tissue paper
Scissors
White paper
Shiny craft foam or cardboard
Paper fasteners
Glitter

1. To make a basic snowflake, draw a circle shape on a piece of tissue paper (*as fig 1*). (Use the bottom of a cup or a small tea-plate as a guide, depending on the size you want.)
2. Cut out, then fold the circle in half, and then in half again. You should now have a curved triangle shape (*as figs 2 and 3*).
3. Cut shapes around the edges: points, triangles, ovals, squares, etc (*as fig 4*).

244

4. To make a small hole in the middle
   of the snowflake, snip
   a tiny bit off the point of your
   triangle. Don't snip too much
   though, as you don't want this
   hole to be too large.

5. Open out, and your first
   snowflake is complete (*as fig 5*).

6. Now repeat using different
   coloured sheets of tissue paper.
   Try to make a few snowflakes
   that are slightly larger, and some
   that are slightly smaller than the
   others. Also cut out a couple of
   snowflakes using plain white
   paper.

7. Finally make one large snowflake
   to go at the back of your
   decoration. Use cardboard for
   this or shiny craft foam if you
   have it.

8. When you have at least half a
   dozen snowflakes, pile them
   on top of one another to make
   a snowflake tower – with the
   largest at the back and the smaller
   ones at the front. Next stick your
   paper fastener through the middle
   of the pile. (You might need a
   grown-up to help with this bit.)

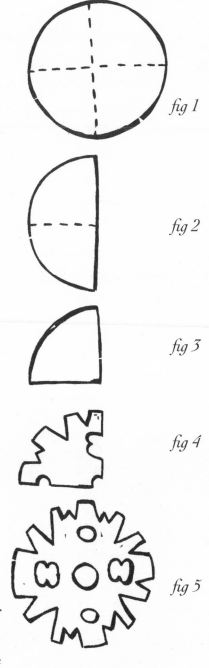

fig 1

fig 2

fig 3

fig 4

fig 5

9. Use your scissors to trim the flakes – make the larger snowflakes spikier, so they stand out a bit more.

10. Next, dribble some glue over the snowflake, putting a blob in the middle to cover the front of your paper fastener, and cover with glitter. Shake off and leave to dry.

You can stick your snowflake decoration on a wrapped-up Christmas present, or make a smaller one to go on the envelope of a special Christmas card.

This design also works really well with flower shapes in the spring.

They started on their carol

Window Snowflakes

So Milly-Molly-Mandy jumped out of bed and looked. "Oh!" she said, staring. "Oh-h!"

For everything outside her little low window was white as white could be, except the sky, which was dark, dirty grey and criss-crossed all over with snowflakes flying down.

Milly-Molly-Mandy Goes Sledging

Even if it doesn't snow this winter, you can make your own snowflakes to hang at the window.

You will need:

White paper

Coloured tissue paper

Decorations: glitter, tinsel or sequins

Glue

1. Make snowflakes in the same way as pages 244–46, but this time use white paper. Now decorate with glitter and sequins, or cut tiny bits off a piece of tinsel and glue them on the flakes.
2. Then cut out a circle the same size as your snowflake from coloured tissue paper.
3. Stick the tissue paper to the back of the snowflake, attach a thread at the top and hang above a window.
4. When the light shines through the tissue paper, it will light up your snowflake beautifully.

Old Christmas-card Makes

Milly-Molly-Mandy is good at making things out of leftovers. When Christmas is finished, ask if you can have some of the old Christmas cards. There are loads of great things you can make from them – just save and store them away for next Christmas!

" PEACE ON EARTH · GOODWILL TO MEN "

Christmas-card gift tags

You will need:
Fancy-edged scissors (if you don't have any, just use
    ordinary scissors)
Old Christmas cards
A hole-punch
Thin ribbon or string
Glitter

1. Look through the Christmas cards and choose the best pictures. Cut them out using your fancy scissors to give them a patterned edge (if you haven't got fancy scissors, just use ordinary ones. You can cut in a pattern later).

2. Cut the tags into whatever shape you want: rectangle, square, circle, triangle or star. If there is any writing on the back of the picture, glue it on to a sheet of cardboard and cut round it to make a backing for your tag.

3. Use a hole-punch to make a hole to thread string or ribbon through.

4. You can decorate your tags with glitter. To make a glittery border, dip the edges of your shape in runny glue and then in glitter. Shake any extra off. Or you can use the glitter to highlight parts of the picture.

5. Leave to dry and your tags are ready to be packed away for next Christmas – just don't forget where you put them!

Christmas boxes

Here's a great way to make a special gift using old Christmas cards. Turn them into Christmas boxes then fill them with goodies to give to your friends and family.

You will need:
Old Christmas cards
A ruler
Pencil
Scissors
Sticky tape

1. Take a card and cut it in half along the fold line. Now you should have two pieces – the half with the picture on it and the greetings part.
2. Now you need to decide what sort of box you want to make.
3. You could make an open tray box, which won't have a lid. Or you could make a box with a lid. Here's how to do both:

Tray box

1. To make a tray box, you put the picture on the inside so that you can see it.
2. Using your ruler, lightly pencil in a margin on the left hand and right hand sides of the picture, and then draw two more margins at the same distance from the top and bottom edges. The margins should probably be about 1 in (2.5 cm) wide, but it depends how deep you'd like your box to be. Wider margins will make a deeper box.
3. The lines you have drawn are your fold lines. Bend and crease all the folds and open the card out again. Then, starting at the beginning of the fold lines on the short sides, cut along the lines at each corner until you reach the pencil line that crosses in the other direction.
4. Now fold up your box, using the cuts to form joints. Secure with sticky tape.
5. Fill with home-made sweets or chocolates – or buy some loose sweets to put in your box. Cover with cellophane and a pretty ribbon.

Lid box

1. To make a box with a lid, follow the same directions as before, but this time make your picture the outside of the box. This will be the lid of your box.

2. You can use the other half of the card – the greetings section – to make the bottom of the box, though you'll have to cover over the writing with a piece of card. Or it may be easier to use a fresh piece of card to make the bottom of your box.

3. Follow the same directions as before, but this time make the margins slightly deeper than you did with the lid – this will allow the bottom of the box to fit snugly under the lid.

4. Now your box is ready to fill with tissue paper and goodies.

Christmas-fairy Peg Dolls

Aunty gave them some fruit-sweets wrapped in coloured papers. Milly-Molly-Mandy and Little-friend-Susan put their sweet-wrappers into their baskets to take home.
Milly-Molly-Mandy Goes for a Picnic

These little dolls are
perfect for perching on the
Christmas tree, and great to
give as gifts.

You will need:
A wooden dolly peg
Felt-tip pens
Fabric circle (about 6 in
    (15 cm) diameter)
Elastic band
Thin sparkly pipe cleaner
    (or glitter to decorate a
    non-sparkly one)
Shiny sweetie wrapper or kitchen foil
Double-sided sticky tape
Silver cardboard (or ordinary cardboard covered in kitchen
    foil)

1. First, draw your doll's face and hair on the dolly peg.
2. Next, make a small hole in the fabric, just big enough to

squeeze over the doll's head. Pull it down and secure with an elastic band. (If you don't have fabric, you could use a paper napkin, a thick tissue or a paper doily.)

3. Make a sash from a folded sweetie wrapper or a piece of folded kitchen foil. Cover the elastic band with this, and secure at the back with double-sided sticky tape.

4. Cut a pair of wings out of the silver cardboard (or plain cardboard covered in kitchen foil) and secure to the back of your doll with double-sided sticky tape.

5. Twist the pipe cleaner around the neck twice for arms. Then peg the doll on to the Christmas tree.

❖ You could also try making a **Christmas angel**. Use white or silver fabric for the skirt and kitchen foil for the sash. Give your doll golden hair made from yellow wool, and make a halo out of an extra-sparkly pipe cleaner twisted into a halo shape and attached to the back of the doll.

❖ Or perhaps you could make a **Santa doll**. Use red crêpe paper for his clothes and hat, cotton wool for his beard and the trimming on his outfit, and black felt for his boots. Don't forget to make him a felt sack too, stuffed with cotton wool to look like presents!

Sweet-treat Dancers

A pretty picture full of dancing ladies made from sweetie wrappers is quick and fun to make – and another great way to use up old sweetie wrappers.

You will need:
Assorted shiny sweetie wrappers
A large sheet of card or paper
Double-sided or ordinary sticky
   tape
Felt-tip pens
Sequins and glue
Larger sheet of cardboard

1. Take a sweetie wrapper and twist it at one end. Leave the other end open. Now you should have a dancing dress shape.
2. Glue this to the sheet of card or paper with the tied end at the top and the loose end below. Use double-sided sticky tape or a small rolled-up bit of ordinary sticky tape.
3. Next draw in your dancer's neck, head, arms and feet. Add a face, some hair and perhaps some evening gloves and jewellery.
4. Use sequins to add some detail to the dresses, or as hair or shoe decorations.

5. Repeat until the whole sheet is covered.
   Try to vary the poses of your dancers —
   some could be holding hands and
   dancing together, others pirouetting or
   standing on tip-toes.

6. When you've finished, you could use a
   thick black pen to outline your dancers
   and make them stand out more.

7. Finally, glue your picture on to a larger
   sheet of cardboard to make a frame.

Salt-dough Decorations

When the weather's too wet to go outside, making salt dough is a great way to while away an afternoon. Once you've made these decorations they'll last for years.

You will need:
2 cups plain flour, plus extra for dusting
1 cup salt
1 cup water
One tablespoon vegetable oil
Biscuit or gingerbread-men cutters
Pencil
Paint and PVA glue for decorating
Ribbon to hang decorations up with

1. Mix the dry ingredients together. Then slowly add the water, followed by the oil.
2. Dust your worktop or pastry board with flour to stop it sticking, then start kneading the dough. You should do this for about 10 minutes, until it starts to feel quite elastic.
3. Next roll the dough out until it's quite thin – about ¼ in (0.5 cm) deep.
4. Use biscuit cutters to make your shapes. Gingerbread men are fun to decorate. Stars and hearts work well too.
5. When you've finished, use a pencil to make a small hole at the top of each shape so that you can hang them up later.

6. Next bake them. Switch your oven on to the lowest setting and bake on baking trays lined with greaseproof paper for between 3 and 4 hours (turning once or twice), until the shapes are fully hardened. Don't be tempted to put them in a hotter oven, as they may crack!
7. You could try microwaving them instead – 2 or 3 minutes should do the trick.
8. When they're ready, leave them to cool.
9. Next is the fun bit – decorating! Use paint mixed with PVA glue to make it stick better. You could also use glitter, glitter glue and sequins.
10. When the shapes are dry, thread a ribbon through the holes and hang on the tree or on door handles.

Stained-glass Paper Pictures

This is a pretty decoration to hang in the window. When the light shines through, the colours light up beautifully.

You will need:
A few shiny sweetie wrappers
2 sheets of coloured cardboard
Scissors
Sticky tape
Ribbon or string to hang your picture

1. Fold a sheet of cardboard in half top to bottom, then again side to side. Now use your scissors to cut a pattern out of the edges, as though you're making a snowflake.
2. When you've finished, unfold the cardboard. Now stick your sweetie wrappers over the holes. Experiment with colours – try using two wrappers at once. Sticky-tape around the edges, not over the holes themselves.
3. Make a frame for your holey card using the other piece of cardboard. You could make this into an arched shape like a church window, or whatever other shape you like.
4. Stick the card with the wrappers into the frame, fasten a loop of ribbon or string on the back and then hang it in the window. Watch and enjoy as the light streams through!

TIP ❅ ❅ ❅

If you don't want to use the "snowflake" method to make the holes, try cutting some Christmassy shapes from your cardboard – trees, crackers or holly.

❅ ❅ ❅

You can read all about Milly-Molly-Mandy and her friends in these four mini story collections!

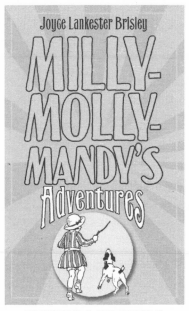

ISBN 978-0-230-75500-0

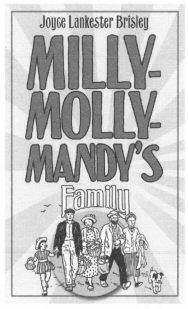

ISBN 978-0-230-75498-0

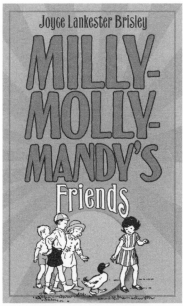

ISBN 978-0-230-75497-3

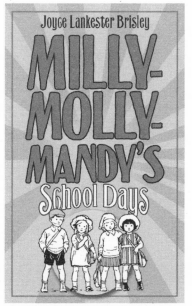

ISBN 978-0-230-75502-4

Joyce Lankester Brisley was born in 1896 and studied art at Lambeth Art School. The first Milly-Molly-Mandy stories were published in 1925 in the *Christian Science Monitor* and such was their popularity that they were published in book form in 1928. An accomplished artist, Brisley designed posters and book jackets as well as illustrating the work of other authors. Joyce Lankester Brisley died in 1978, but Milly-Molly-Mandy's popularity lives on.

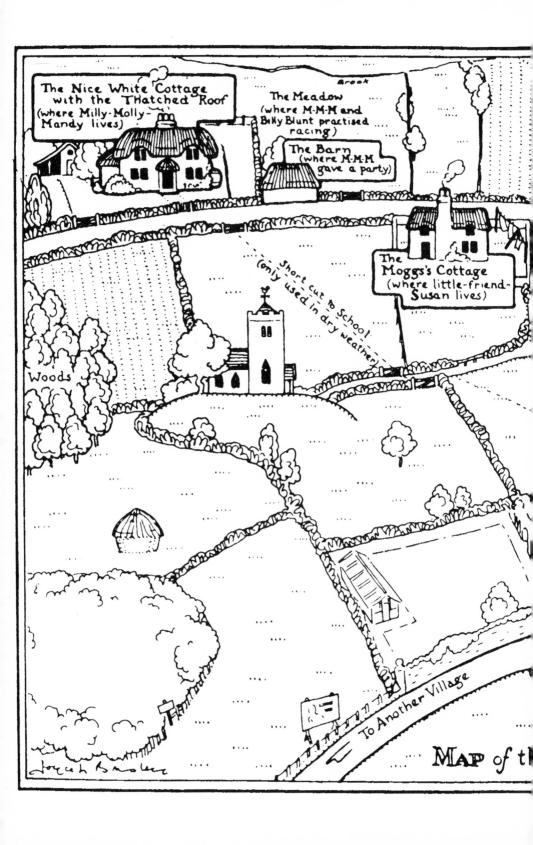